Power Shift

The New Rules of Engagement

**Discover What Happens
When an Irresistible Force
Meets an Influential Leader**

Editor: Gina E. Morgan

Printed in the United States of America, Canada and the United Kingdom

ISBN: 978-0-9861314-0-0

QuinStar Publishing – Dallas, Texas

Contents

INTRODUCTION   vii

CHAPTER ONE

Leadership Myths and Trends   1

CHAPTER TWO

The Khan Conundrum   19

CHAPTER THREE

Lessons from a Maverick   27

CHAPTER FOUR

Game Changers   35

CHAPTER FIVE

Getting the Best from People   45

CHAPTER SIX

The Performance Platform   61

CHAPTER SEVEN

Enforced Versus Legitimate Power   81

CHAPTER EIGHT

The Litmus Test   89

CHAPTER NINE

There's a New Kid in Town   97

CHAPTER TEN

Mindset and Energy   121

CHAPTER ELEVEN

Authentic Leadership   137

CHAPTER TWELVE

A System for Success   151

ABOUT THE AUTHORS   169

BIBLIOGRAPHY   175

INDEX   178

INTRODUCTION

In the 30 years we have worked with leaders, entrepreneurs and teams as trainers, consultants and key personnel coaches, we have witnessed many changes. Not just in technological advances, but in the way people  relate to one another and to the world. We have seen shifts in the marketplace, in customer expectations, in requirements for employee satisfaction, in change management methods, in processes, procedures, and leadership styles. We have seen workplace philosophies and methods evolve, and sometimes devolve, over time. We have seen the effects of four generations in the workplace and of diversity challenges that have arisen from global connectivity. We have seen the effect on leaders and their people of too much change in too short a time. Through it all, our focus has been on helping leaders get the best from themselves and their people so they are equipped to handle it all.

Until about fifteen years ago, most leaders felt capable of managing most of the challenges they encountered so helping them move their people through change and to higher levels of performance was relatively simple. Things began to shift in the late-eighties with the emergence of the internet. The pace of change picked up and there was a lot for leaders and their people to learn in order to keep up. Baby Boomers and many Traditionalists made the technology transition fairly easily. Transitioning to a new way of working with people, especially the newer generations, has been another story.

Around the turn of the century, as Generation X began populating workplaces, leaders began lamenting the extreme departure of this new generation from the norm, and expressing concern about their behaviors in the workplace.

As a behavioral psychologist and researcher, Sherry and her team began researching this new generation in order to address the concerns leaders continued to express. The research continued for twelve years and carried over into the Millennial generation. It focused on three areas: (1) the core values of Generation X and Millennials, (2) the mindset and behaviors driven by those values, and (3) how these fit with prevailing business and leadership models. Core values were studied because they don't change over time. The core values of each generation have always been the drivers and sustainers of change. It was in studying the core values of these two generations in relation to previous generations and current business and leadership practices that the first glimpse of an inevitable power shift emerged.

At the same time, Marc was traveling the globe teaching leaders a new model of leadership and was hearing the same laments and getting the same kinds of questions from leaders everywhere he went: "What do we do about these young people? How do we get them to follow protocol?"

As we looked further, we found hundreds of articles about this ever-growing problem, and volumes of research, which validated our observation that this was no small problem. We collectively began gathering information from leaders and from members of every generation currently found in the workplace; Traditionalists, Baby Boomers, Generation X, and Millennials.

What we found was a game-changing zeitgeist that is global in size and currently immeasurable in scope. A zeitgeist is the defining spirit or mood of a particular period in history which is driven by the ideas and beliefs of the time. Those that are a radical departure from previously held ideas and beliefs generally result in a shift that brings with it dramatic changes. The emerging zeitgeist is creating just such a shift, and one critically important part of that shift is the fulcrum of power.

This appears to be the most dramatic shift in centuries, and one that is likely to last for at least fifty years. Leaders cannot escape this power shift, but they can influence it if they have the right tools and understanding. Providing these is the goal of this book.

Power Shift is essentially a SWOT analysis of leadership today and into the future. It provides leaders with the information they need to evaluate their strengths, weaknesses, opportunities and threats so they are fully aware of the risks involved in continuing along the old leadership path, the challenges they are likely to encounter as they adopt a new and better model, and the huge benefits of meeting those challenges. From a place of deeper awareness, leaders can expand their strengths, minimize weaknesses, and take full advantage of the great opportunities that lie before them.

The shift has already begun and as it gains momentum, it will have a dramatic impact on everything from societies to governments to business on every level. Drastic change in the workplace is not a matter of if; only when. No leader can afford to miss this reality. Those who fail to see and prepare for it may well find themselves without a job and perhaps without a company in the not too distant future.

By 2025 Millennials will dominate the workplace and, since core values remain relatively constant over time, learning to meet Millennials where they live is not an option for organizations that want to remain viable into the future. The time is short. To effectively manage this change and get the best from the emerging workforce, leaders must begin preparing right now. Drastic change can be scary, but it can also be an opportunity for tremendous growth.

The goal of this book is threefold:

To present the scary facts so leaders are fully aware and alert.

To present the opportunities that lie beyond and within the great power shift so leaders can ride that wave to unprecedented success.

To provide knowledge and tools leaders can use to forge a new, more beneficial and profitable path faster and with the greater ease.

We are on the threshold of a major shift; one that is inescapable and filled with both risk and opportunity. Awareness of both is the key to leading change we can all embrace.

"The greatest danger in times of turbulence is not the turbulence – It is to act with yesterday's logic."

Peter Drucker

CHAPTER ONE
LEADERSHIP MYTHS AND TRENDS

We are at a place in history where something really big is happening. An irresistible force is pressing hard against an entrenched immovable object and, as any physicist will tell you, *something has got to give.* Physicists will also tell you that when an irresistible force meets an immovable object, what always gives is the *immovable object.* No matter how big or how powerful the object, it eventually succumbs to the irresistible force.

Powerful generational values; core beliefs which drive choices, behaviors, attitudes, actions, performance, and outcomes are the irresistible force leaders and managers are always up against. Core values have driven every power shift throughout history and, while they can be managed when understood, they cannot be changed and leaders who try generally find themselves quickly losing control.

What makes the coming shift so powerful is the size, global reach and instant connectivity of the Millennial generation. No generation before them has been larger, not even the Baby Boom generation which led significant societal and organizational change, and no generation has ever had the level of awareness or power which global connectivity has given Millennials.

The changes created by previous generations were more like wind or water slowly wearing down a great stone mountain. That kind of change allows plenty of time to adjust. With Millennials, the change is more like a laser-beam focused on steel. The change is fast and furious and even steel is no match.

In organizations, the immovable object is inflexible leaders clinging to outdated rules and management practices which have become as impractical as rotting logs in a tsunami and those who insist on clinging to them are just as likely to drown.

One of the most damaging beliefs in business today is the idea that continuing to build on the model of a bygone era will yield satisfactory results now and in the future. Even in slower, more predictable times the hierarchical model was not a good one. It stifled innovation and fed command and control cultures which are centuries old carry-overs from kingdoms and fiefdoms.

Industrial-age tycoons were able to adopt that model only because physical labor was the machine that drove organizations in the agricultural and industrial ages and enforced servitude was sufficient to get a result. Things began to shift when the world moved from the industrial age to the Baby Boom driven information age in the late seventies. In the forty-plus years since, a lot has changed, but the changes Baby Boomers influenced are nothing compared to what leaders are about to face.

The changes occurring now will bring with them the greatest power shift the world has seen since science shifted the over-arching power of religion. Leadership models were forced into drastic change back then because what everyone had once accepted without question was no longer viable. It is that same world-changing shift today's leaders are about to experience because Millennials have a whole new view of the world and of what matters.

To meet them where they live, as we must, leaders need to be awake, aware and prepared. Clinging to the old management model has cost organizations billions of dollars and hobbled companies in ways few imagine. A study of the management practices of now defunct organizations such as Montgomery Ward, Wang Labs, Circuit City, Polaroid, TWA, WorldCom, Comp USA, and hundreds of others should provide sufficient proof that what used to work no longer does. Even large, well funded organizations such as those once listed in the Standard and Poor 500 index (established in 1957) have not survived. Just 74 (15%) of Standard and Poor's original top rated companies remain and many of those, such as JC Penney, are struggling.

Avoiding such destruction isn't as hard as the leaders of these now defunct or struggling companies make it seem, but to get off a destructive path requires new information, expanded awareness, and a lot more openness to alternatives than many entrenched leaders are willing to entertain.

A good place to begin is with an exploration of leadership itself and an examination of persistent and generally false beliefs (myths) that continue to impact the way organizations view, select and groom leaders. As with most myths, these have not served the business community well and many companies have paid a very high price for adhering to them.

As the power shift gains momentum, these myths are likely to create even greater challenges for organizations that cling to them. This is by no means an exhaustive list; just the ones we keep running into and find to be detrimental to organizational development and growth. With each myth we present the distorted lens through which people generally view reality, the behavior that view induces, the result of the behavior, the current trend and facts that can dispel the myth.

MYTH #1: Leaders must control people to get results

LENS: People don't like to work and are not self-motivated to act. Leaders must therefore monitor and control their actions to ensure results.

BEHAVIOR: Theory X, authoritarian leadership style; tell versus connect and engage; push for results; make sure people are sequestered in a central place where they can be watched; don't bother getting to know employees on a personal level because that has no real value; focus on external motivators.

RESULT: Disengaged employees who are over-stressed, risk averse and under-performing. Such employees adopt dependent behavior and obey out of fear. Motivation must be regularly induced and enticements increased. Intrinsic motivation is lacking.

TREND: Resistance is high among managers and leaders as they struggle to bring the new generations into line. The inability to manage Gen X and Millennials using the old model is creating wide gaps in communication, increasing stress and stress related consequences, and creating conditions that are costing time, money and energy. It's a no-win situation. When communication, connection and consideration are lacking, the approach of the newer generations is to simply walk out the door. They continue to exit the corporate world in droves and companies continue to search for talent, never realizing they are just spinning their wheels and creating the very conditions that keep the best and brightest from staying.

REALITY: With the new attitudes and values of the emerging workforce, the authoritarian style is not working and never will. Those who cling to this style will find themselves with greater challenges than they will be able to handle as Millennials dominate the workplace in the next ten to twelve years. This myth is what keeps the Theory X management model alive.

The fact is, neither Theory X nor Theory Y work well as stand-alone styles. Authoritarian styles don't work well because very few people want to be controlled. This style has always been a demotivator. Most people actively resist being controlled. They dig in their heels and do only as much as they must to keep their job. The authoritarian style should not be confused with strong leadership, however. Most people are followers who want and value strong leadership as long as they also have some freedom and flexibility within the set boundaries.

Where Theory X managers are too controlling, Theory Y managers often fail to lead strongly enough. People want and need clear boundaries which come from clear, concise and complete communications. When people are clear about what's expected of them and believe the leader has faith in their ability to achieve the goal without micro-managing; when they have clear boundaries to work within and the freedom to decide how they will get the job done, most will rise to meet the challenge.

Today's workforce meets challenges so well that under the right conditions and leadership, huge empires have been built almost overnight. Empires like Google, FaceBook, LinkedIn, Starbucks and Zappos have leapt to the top in earnings and influence in record time even as problems keep mounting for businesses with leaders who continue to cling to the old ways.

While old school companies are laying people off and tightening their budgets in an attempt to hold their bottom line, those using the new leadership model are thriving. And it isn't just the fresh, new companies. A few well established companies have successfully adopted the new leadership model too; companies like Apple, Bridgestone, Adecco Group, Publix and Costco.

Southwest Airlines is a successful company that was ahead of its time. Herb Kelleher, the founder of Southwest Airlines, was a visionary who saw the value in leading differently well before it was a necessary or even popular concept. Kelleher was once asked if he was concerned that the competition was looking at his model and attempting to emulate it. He replied that he was not the least bit concerned because his competition was looking at *processes* and *procedures*, not at the real secret to Southwest's success—its *people*. The *deeper secret* is Kelleher's leadership style and the way he structured his company. Most people can be motivated to exceptional performance and most are willing to follow a great leader. Herb Kelleher was a great leader. He created a people-centric culture first, then built an infrastructure to support it, systems to facilitate it, and a succession plan to ensure those who followed him would be great leaders as well.

To use the metaphor of Jim Collins, author of *Good to Great*, Kelleher first got the right people on the bus (in his case, the plane) and in the right seats, checked to ensure his vehicle was sound and would get his people where he (and they) wanted to go, and then got the plane in the air (literally and figuratively). He also made sure that his people continued to enjoy the trip and that the next "pilot" would be just as good as he was.

Companies like Southwest Airlines prove it's possible to have an organization filled with engaged, committed, loyal employees who support the company's vision, values, mission and goals; employees who are dedicated to serving their employer and their customers well.

MYTH # 2: Leaders are born not developed

LENS: I don't have to improve my skills. I already know how to lead. I am a born leader and I have led in other arenas.

BEHAVIOR: People with such an attitude usually don't participate in training or development programs and don't encourage others to develop leadership skills either. They have an arrogance and sense of self-importance about them that demotivates employees and causes the workforce to disengage. To this "leader" all problems are the fault of their people and to fix the problems, the *people* need to be fixed. Rarely, if ever, do they look at the real source of the problem, which is *always* leadership. As the leader goes, so go their followers.

RESULT: Ineffective leadership, disengaged employees, low morale, departmental silos, distrust, poor results, high resentment, high illness and absenteeism, and very low productivity.

TREND: Resistance to changing outdated leadership and management models is still high in most organizations. Historically, people resist change until the pain of continuing the old behaviors exceeds the pain of effort to change. When the pain doesn't get high enough to induce positive change in an organization early enough, the organization falls apart. Today there are more organizations failing to change and falling apart than making the change and taking quantum leaps forward. Though the early adopters have a huge advantage, as long as leaders assume they know all they need to know and avoid learning the new, more viable methods, the trend toward demise will continue.

REALITY: People are born with the *capacity* to lead, but not the *ability*. These are two completely different things. With continual changes in the marketplace and changes in the attitudes of employees and customers, continuous development is critically important for everyone and especially for leaders. Capacity is raw potential. Ability is raw potential developed over time through learning and experience to the point of effective application.

A classic example of this is emotional intelligence (EQ or EI). We are born with the tendency to manage stress either aggressively or passively (fight, flight or freeze). These tendencies are managed, if at all, in either healthy or unhealthy ways. Passive-aggressiveness is an unhealthy adaption where assertiveness is a healthy adaption (see *illustration 1.1*). Naturally bold people (extroverts) default to aggression. Naturally reserved or cautious people (introverts) default to passivity. Because most people who aspire to lead are extroverted types, they tend to default to aggression. If that tendency is not managed in a healthy way, they get more and more aggressive as stress goes up, or they resort to passive-aggressive manipulation, neither of which makes for great leadership.

The healthy adaption, assertiveness, is a *learned* skill. Though we are all born with the *capacity* to be assertive, no one comes into the world with this skill already developed. In fact, years of study reveals that only 12% of the population has learned healthy assertiveness skills. The other 88% are reacting aggressively, passively, or passive-aggressively, all of which are poor leadership approaches.

Many people mistake aggressiveness for assertiveness and they are two very different behavioral styles. People who default to aggression are concerned only with getting what they want in the moment. People who

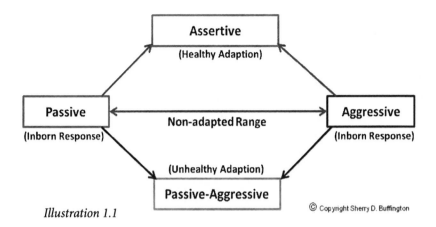

Illustration 1.1   © Copyright Sherry D. Buffington

have learned assertiveness look at the bigger picture. They consider the effect on all parties involved and the long-term effect.

Which of the coping styles we use is determined by intention, attitude and approach. For example, there are people who have the *capacity* to be a leader, but not the intention, so leadership is essentially off their radar. Or as a leader, an individual may have the *intent* to serve others or the intent to serve self. An individual may have the intent to be effective (take a disciplined path) or to do things the easiest way possible (be undisciplined). What kind of leader an individual is, and even whether the person aspires to be a leader, is colored by these intents.

Imagine how ineffective someone born with the *capacity* to be a leader, but with the *intent* to take the easy path and serve only self would be. What do you suppose that individual's attitude would be? What do you suppose the approach might be? What kind of leader do you imagine this individual would become?

Intention is generally values based and usually learned before the age of 12. Once developed, we typically don't change our values unless we experience a significant emotional event; something that causes us to back up and re-evaluate what we have taken for granted up to that point.

> To be a great leader requires learning, and the leaders of today need more learning than any who came before them. To positively influence the new generations, leaders need a completely different mindset and completely different tools than leaders of the past used.

Effectively tapping into intrinsic motivators is one of the things that can produce significant emotional responses, which is why one of our primary goals as consultants and trainers is to help leaders, managers and key personnel tap into their own intrinsic motivators, and learn ways to discover and activate them in their employees. People who are intrinsically motivated toward a goal are *intent* on achieving that goal and they are generally unstoppable.

Though there are people born with the *capacity* to lead, to be a great leader requires learning, and the leaders of today need more learning than any who came before them. They will also need a completely different mindset and completely different tools than those used in the past to influence the new generations. Lacking a new set of skills and clear intentions, they will have no motivation to inspire a new and very different workforce to the excellence the new generations are quite capable of producing.

In the most successful and profitable companies, leaders see themselves as a member of their team and their role as that of supporting the team's efforts. They participate in the same training employees get and more. They make it a point to know what their employees know and to connect and communicate with them on their level. In the most successful companies, there is no ivory tower and no king or dictator.

The *intent* of a great and influential leader is to help others be their very best. They take the responsible, disciplined path and make the hard choices, but they also give their people the tools and support they need to be great. They provide clear and specific boundaries which apply to everyone equally and allow a lot of freedom for employees to do their best work within those boundaries. They take the time to know their people so they know their employees' capabilities and place them in jobs where the leader can trust them to perform. They convey to their people that they value, trust and believe in them and they reach out with the intent of redirecting rather than correcting. Correction implies the other is wrong and the one doing the correcting is right. Redirection implies the other is simply off the path temporarily and that with a purposeful adjustment they can get back on track.

The *attitude* of an influential leader is one of realizing there is always room for improvement. They continually take steps to develop themselves so they can better serve their people.

The *approach* of an influential leader is one of continually seeking ways to help their people reach their highest potential and be their absolute best both on and off the job so they provide their people with continual training to ensure they are always growing.

MYTH #3: All good leaders are bold, extroverted types

LENS: I can determine who will be a great leader by looking at their personality or their observable behaviors.

BEHAVIOR: Rely on impressions in an interview or use basic personality assessments such as Meyers-Briggs or DISC to validate their assumptions. Fail to consider other types when making a hiring decision.

RESULT: The wrong people are put into important leadership roles which can cost companies millions of dollars in lost productivity and severance packages when those who appear to be great leaders on the surface are, in fact, not. Worse than the direct financial cost is the indirect costs where the whole workforce is demotivated, turnover is high, morale low and the entire company set back, sometimes by years. History is replete with examples of companies where the wrong leader has taken a once healthy company and put it out of business in the space of a few years.

The number one reason why employees leave a company is poor leadership, and those who leave first are typically the high performers. According to a *Gallup* poll of more than a million employees, the number one reason given in exit polls for leaving was a "bad boss or supervisor." *Gallup* concluded, "People leave managers not companies. In the end, turnover is mostly a manager issue." The effect of poor management is widely felt and costly in ways not often considered. *Gallup* found that poorly managed work groups are on average 50 percent less productive and 44 percent less profitable than well-managed groups.

TREND: Currently the trend remains heavily weighted toward the value of extroversion as an indicator of leadership effectiveness. Most top level leaders are extroverted types and simply assume people like them will be good leaders. This trend is still holding strong, but may begin to shift as awareness of the extreme importance of the deeper, less easily observed factors, such as development levels, reactionary patterns, coping styles, and tolerance levels, are revealed. The assessment called the *CORE Multidimensional Awareness Profile* (CORE MAP) accurately measures all of these vitally important factors, which is why we use this tool.

REALITY: There is a lot more to leadership effectiveness than basic personality and observable traits. Though introverted types rarely seek a top level position, they can be highly effective leaders on other levels. Introverts actually make excellent leaders with the right training, and extroverts can be highly ineffective leaders without the right training and a full understanding and consideration of human nature.

As a side note: the type that most frequently seeks leadership roles (the type identified as Commander on the CORE Profile) often profiles on other assessments as introverts when, in reality they are extroverts who extrovert their energy through *action* rather than interaction. This anomaly is frequently seen as a result of the incorrect assumption made with other assessments that all extroverts are sociable. The correct definition of extroversion is *a bold approach*. The type identified as Entertainer on the CORE Profile is the type that is sociable and bold when it comes to people. Commanders tend to dislike social situations and avoid them unless there is a specific reason for being there, but they take bold action to make things happen and are quite bold with people in business settings, sports or other action oriented settings.

MYTH #4: People who have led before know how to lead

LENS: Leadership is leadership. People who have been effective leaders in other organizations already have what it takes to lead.

BEHAVIOR: Lack of due diligence in making sure the candidate has the right stuff for the organization's particular environment or industry. Inattention to, or lack of awareness of the need for continuous improvement.

RESULT: Leaders are often chosen based on past performance with little attention to the environment or industry they came from, which can result in choosing a leader that is doomed to fail in the new environment or industry. Poorly chosen leaders lead to disengaged employees, high distrust, low morale, and lost profits.

TREND: As the attitudes of employees shift, ineffective leaders are more and more stressed, and more and more ineffective, and their ineffectiveness is more visible than ever before. Performance studies consistently show that motivation and stress are inversely correlated; motivation and effectiveness drop off dramatically as stress levels increase. Organizations the world over are feeling the effects of excessive stress and many have no idea what to do about it or how to shift this unhealthy dynamic.

It is this growing tide of stress and unrest that we are focused on helping leaders and their people manage for overall organizational success. This is a much broader undertaking than most leaders assume and, with the right focus and training, is also a lot *faster* and *easier* than most imagine.

REALITY: Though there are certainly specific types who seek leadership, leadership is a skill, not a birthright. Every aspiring leader needs training to learn effective strategies and how to motivate and inspire people, and every leader needs to fit the environment, culture and industry they are in.

MYTH #5: People don't like change and have to be forced to make the changes necessary for company growth

LENS: Leaders must push employees through change and only the leaders need to know where the change is leading. The less employees know when change is massive, the less likely they are to panic. Employees only need to understand what's immediately in front of them.

BEHAVIOR: Force and, if necessary, coerce or manipulate to get people to comply.

RESULT: People dig in their heels and resist, partly to maintain their dignity and partly because moving into unknown territory is scary. No one reacts well to being pushed, and bolder employees are inclined to push back creating friction and distracting the entire team from the goal of moving through change successfully. The overall result is an adversarial relationship that wastes precious time and resources. Fear of the unknown is our one inborn fear and will always stop or slow action.

TREND: The focus today is on improving processes, procedures and methods for facilitating change. Training, consulting and coaching is primarily focused on increasing "hard" skills directed at better managing processes and procedures. The needs and interests of the people and personal development are considered "soft" or non-essential skills and are less often invested in.

REALITY: Change management is *always* about people. As the workforce shifts from more traditional workers to the more independently minded Generation X and Millennial workers, trying to force change through process management will get more and more difficult and many change initiatives will fail. People with values of independence and life-balance must be led differently than those who were taught to respect authority and follow the rules.

Unless leaders learn to lead the emerging workforce in alignment with their needs and values, the changes necessary to survive and thrive in today's fast-changing world of business will get more and more difficult to manage. Organizations today must understand and take care of their employees in ways most have not yet considered if they are to keep top performers and stay abreast of the rapid changes in today's world economy.

We now live in the age of information and technology, both of which require brain-power as opposed to manual labor. And, while manual labor can be forced, thinking and creativity cannot. The harder you push people to think or innovate, the less they do. This is *not* stubbornness, bad attitude, push-back, or sabotage as many managers believe; it's the nature of the brain. Under stress, the brain goes from thinking (cerebral activity) to reactivity (the primitive brain response). This is a natural response, not an intention. No matter how well-intentioned, when the thinking aspects of the brain shut down, creativity shuts down with it. Bottom line: the harder you push for creativity, the less you get.

MYTH #6: Employees should be informed of upcoming changes on a "need to know" basis

LENS: Too much information too soon will lead to unnecessary worry, which could increase fear, lower productivity and distract employees from our current goals.

BEHAVIOR: Being secretive; avoiding conversations with inquisitive employees; lying about what leadership really knows; presuming that, with information, people will take advantage of the situation or become over-whelmed; under-estimating employee resilience and capacity.

RESULT: We all have one innate fear; fear of the unknown. When the direction change is headed is unclear, fear is a natural result and most people do not go willingly into fear inducing situations. When leaders fail to convey information about upcoming changes to their people, they inadvertently foster a climate of distrust, fear and resistance, which actually creates the very thing they fear; high anxiety and low productivity. As shown in *Illustration 1.2* communication and productivity are correlated. The effect of staggered or delayed communication is delayed productivity and the longer it is delayed, the less likely it will return to full productivity. The sooner employees know what is going on, what to expect and where the company is headed, the sooner they can return to productivity.

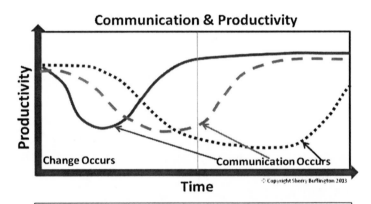

The effect of communication on productivity depends on the timing. The earlier effective communication occurs, the sooner productivity returns to pre-change levels.

Illustration 1.2

In any change event, senior management (solid line) will experience and resolve frustration, confusion and loss of productivity faster than middle level managers (dashed line) who, in turn, experience and resolve these faster than the general workforce (dotted line). The reason: senior managers are privy to key information in the change process earlier than each successive group which allows them to find solutions to personal and organizational issues and then move back up the productivity scale sooner. Without a system to manage the process, fear of the unknown and the need to self-protect creates a breeding ground for unmanaged stress and disengagement. As stress goes up, productivity goes down. ***Bottom line: The earlier effective communication occurs on every level, the sooner employees will return to pre-change levels of productivity.***

TREND: The need-to-know approach is still practiced in many companies and it is unhealthy. It leads to increased anxiety, resistance, confusion and lowered productivity. The trend among the emerging workforce is to walk out the door of organizations where transparency and mutual respect are lacking, and they see failure to inform as disrespectful. The correlation between effective communication and productivity is an unmistakable one which follows a predictable path.

REALITY: All people can navigate change if they know what to expect. For change to be accepted, leaders must communicate clearly, early and often. Otherwise, fear of the unknown is the driver and results in avoidance, self-protection and huge losses in productivity and profit.

Change and the Components of Flow

According to Mihaly Csikszentmihalyi, professor, researcher and author of *Flow: The Psychology of Optimal Experience* (2008), an experience that is at once demanding and rewarding leads to the optimal state called flow where we are functioning at our highest potential. Change is, by its very nature, demanding. It is up to the leader to make sure it is also rewarding, and the way to do that is to keep the line of communication open so people know where the change is leading and what's in it for them to help move it along.

Motivation occurs when we are stretching our boundaries toward a relatively *predictable* outcome. No one ever purposefully moves toward confusion and where communication is absent or lacking, confusion is inevitable. It is confusion and fear that cause people to dig in their heels, resist change, leave, or take advantage of a situation.

MYTH #7: All people are motivated by money and perks. That's what drives performance

LENS: These employers believe people work primarily for money and perks so don't believe they need to know them on a deeper level. They believe that as long as they pay people what the job and market requires, they will be able to attract and keep top talent. They believe a good compensation plan and occasional bonuses are all that's needed to keep employees motivated.

BEHAVIOR: Leaders don't bother to connect to employees on any level other than money, perks and rewards. Instead of spending time with their people getting to know what matters to them, such leaders spend time trying to decide what the next salary increase should be, whether and when to give bonuses, and what the next recognition program or product should be. They spend their time meeting with vendors to decide what to buy next. A new insurance plan? A cool cup or paperweight with a motivational phrase? A plaque for the wall or award to display? In reality, it doesn't matter much what the chosen "incentive" is. When the leader's behaviors don't validate what the company promotes, the promotion is actually a demotivator.

RESULT: Effectiveness remains low because money in exchange for work is an *expectation*, not a motivator. Money without intrinsic rewards can actually suppress the natural human drive for doing meaningful work.

TREND: In organizations where money is considered the motivator, the new workforce (Gen X and Millennials) are walking out the door because money is *not* a motivator for them. Meaning and feeling connected are.

REALITY: Once a person's basic needs are handled, additional money is a low level, short-term motivator in comparison to appreciation and recognition, genuine caring and involvement on the part of leaders. Money can actually be a demotivator if, for instance, employees are given a bonus for doing a good job one year and then no bonus or a smaller bonus is given the next year. This is especially demotivating if employees feel their work was equal to or better than the year before. Extrinsic motivation is always difficult and increasingly expensive to sustain.

MYTH #8: People who try to lead with caring rather than control and logic are generally weak and ineffective

LENS: You can't be your employees' buddy. Employees take advantage of such leaders and then it's really the people, not the so-called leader, running the show.

BEHAVIOR: The leadership style becomes directive rather than inclusive even if the directive style is contrary to the leader's natural and authentic style.

RESULT: The leader is not connected to their people and has no emotional currency to bring out the best in their people or help them get things done. Employees are disengaged and uncommitted because they don't receive the care, trust, and commitment they need from their leader. Motivation is driven by *emotion* and where emotions are lacking, so too is the *engine* that drives motivation and commitment. Caring leaders tend to be highly effective because they are regularly refueling the motivation engine by connecting to their people at an emotional level.

TREND: The old and, unfortunately, prevailing idea is that caring and other emotions do not belong in the workplace. The new trend, and one that needs to spread a lot faster, is a connected, collaborative approach that is not possible without genuine caring. The emerging workforce insists on a collaborative environment and will not stay in a company where caring and collaboration are lacking.

REALITY: In the companies listed as the best companies to work for, the number one attribute named by employees is caring. Where caring is lacking, the people are disconnected and disengaged. Disengaged people are not productive. Bottom line: caring equals productivity.

Unless caring is a key component of leadership as the workforce shifts, companies will continue to get less than 100% from their people and to lose their best workers. The time it takes for an employee to decide to jump ship will continue to get shorter as the new generations dominate the workforce. This will create a situation where companies without caring leaders will be constantly searching for talent.

The Two Sides of Jack Welch

Even the most effective leaders often have blind spots. Jack Welch, former CEO of General Electric, has been the model of great leadership for many years. The term MBWA (Management by Walking Around) was coined around Welch's habit of walking around and visiting with his employees. He was accessible to them and they knew it. He understood that leadership was about people. Welch once observed, "Before you are a leader, success is all about growing yourself. When you become a leader, success is all about growing others." So far, so good.

On the other side of that shiny coin was Welch's habit of *firing* workers in the bottom 10% of productivity every year. Welch is proud of that decision and still recommends it to other leaders, but let's look at the possible effect this can have on *all* employees. Imagine working really hard to do your best yet knowing that if you don't remain in the top 90% all year, every year, you will be fired—even if you fall short by a mere 0.1%. Imagine knowing that getting fired has nothing to do with your dedication or effectiveness because *somebody* has to fall into that bottom 10% and since you have no way to measure how others are doing, you never know where you stand.

Even if you happen to fall into the top percentages, the fear that someday, for some reason, there may come a time when you fall short would keep you vigilant—and stressed. You might work really hard to try to stay in the top 90%, but what do you suppose your stress levels would be? It's a known fact that as stress goes up, motivation and effectiveness go down. Summarily firing the bottom 10% is not a good formula for building a high performance workforce.

Great leadership requires more than just knowing what your people are doing and great employees are not just those over-achievers who churn out the numbers every year. Sometimes a company's most valuable employees are those who are supporting the high performers. Their numbers might not look all that impressive, but without them the numbers of the high performers might not look too great either.

The most valuable asset an organization can have is intrinsically motivated people and routinely firing a percentage of employees based on arbitrary numbers is no way to motivate. It's actually a very poor management practice and one that certainly won't work with the Millennials. They are great at organizing movements that inspire entire departments to walk out the door when they perceive injustice or unfairness.

One large organization in Dallas lost its entire IT department because the department manager refused to collaborate or listen to their ideas. The entire department walked out and started their own company. This happens so frequently in Silicon Valley in California that the word on the street is that "techies" often change jobs without ever having to change their carpool. Imagine the cost of losing an entire department all at once.

On the other side of the coin, Millennials are also great at spreading the word about companies that treat their employees and customers right, and about products and services they like which often leads to meteoric growth for those companies.

Millennials are going to share information and take one another's recommendations. What they share depends in great part on what organizational leaders convey.

> *"The challenge is not just to build a company that can endure; but to build one that is worthy of enduring."*
>
> James C. Collins

CHAPTER TWO
The Khan Conundrum

Change is hard and clinging to the familiar is easy—up to a point. The best strategies on Earth lose their effectiveness and can even move into the realm of harmful when new information and attitudes render the old obsolete. A perfect case in point is Genghis Khan, the greatest warrior leader of his time. Many tales have been told of Khan and his victories. Many organizations have taken Khan's team-based conquering strategies and sought to adapt them to their organization, and many have found that they don't work as expected. There's a very good reason why.

Khan's strategies were highly effective in his time and environment. He and his descendents ruled for more than a hundred years (1206 -1330). Using Khan's methods, Mongols devastated much larger troops and better supplied armies. In uncivilized cultures where brutality is still acceptable, Khan's methods still get results, but only for awhile. They don't work in the long run even in uncivilized societies and they don't work at all where civility is expected.

The fate of Khan and his armies provide a lens into the future of today's hierarchical corporations which continue to function from the obsolete command and control model and are unwilling to consider how new information, new systems, new strategies and new values inevitably doom the old.

Mongol training was based on interdependence and reinforced through specific training tactics. Khan's army trained for three months each year they were not at war. The high point of this training was a massive hunt called a nerge. In it, they practiced the strategy of encirclement that became the hallmark of all Mongol military operations, and which proved unbeatable on the battlefield for quite some time.

The nerge was a method where thousands of horsemen gathered along a starting line that spanned 80 to 100 miles. At Khan's signal the entire group, fully armed for battle, rode forward at a walk. Over several weeks, the tightly coordinated cavalry swept before it all the wild game it encountered. Then on the Khan's command, the flanks would turn and ride toward each other forming a great circle and trapping all the game for hundreds of square miles. Riders were forbidden to poach anything during the nerge and supreme disgrace fell on any man who allowed some beast to escape. Throughout the exercise officers rode behind shouting orders according to the directions of Khan.

Mongol tradition required that the leader demonstrate his hunting prowess before his men so Khan made sure he took the best game. Until Khan had all he wanted, the soldiers could not begin harvesting the game they had gathered. Through this exercise, the Mongol army learned the discipline, coordination and trust in their ability to conquer which was necessary to press an attack over a vast area. The lessons learned in the nerge were then transferred to conquering enemies. Though the nerge was simply a common nomadic hunting practice given a military spin, it created a highly mobile and disciplined cavalry that regularly defeated armies three to five times its size. Apparently, the men thought the lessons they learned and the game they were able to take was sufficient because apparently no one challenged the legitimacy of Khan's practice of taking the best game to prove his ability to lead in spite of the fact that killing already corralled game isn't much of a feat.

Speed of action and a generous reward system were deciding differences between the Mongols and their opponents and played important roles in Khan's victories. At a time when European aristocrats would wait weeks for a letter from a neighboring ruler, Genghis Khan would have the information he needed down to the most mundane detail within days because of the emphasis the Mongols placed on teamwork and communication. Using a promotion system that rewarded excellence and took full advantage of the European armies' aristocratic structure, Khan was able to put together the most effective army the world had ever witnessed. The reward system was allowing the Mongols to pillage and plunder conquered territories and keep whatever they pillaged.

It's easy to see how an organizational leader could look at Khan's strategies and see them, with a few minor adjustments to the reward system, as ideal. Open pillaging and plundering doesn't work in a civilized world, but some of the more modern reward systems used today are not too far advanced. It is not uncommon for leaders with this mindset to scoop up the best rewards, taking the lion's share of profits and perks and distributing the remains to the troops.

Though Kahn's conquests make a remarkable story and illustrates what can happen when someone decides to stop doing things the way they have always been done, his methods should be viewed, not as a model to follow, but as a cautionary tale. As long as the tools of battle remained the same, Khan's strategies worked and the armies using them were victorious. But then new information came; new tools; new strategies; a new awareness, and the armies which insisted upon continuing to use Khan's strategies based on the fact that they worked well in the past, began to fall. Other armies gained intelligence on the strategies Mongol armies used and changed their tactics. They developed more modern tools such as long range cannons and guns and were soon able to conquer the once unconquerable.

Khan did a lot right, yet when his opponents became aware of his tactics and developed new innovations his tactics were ultimately rendered obsolete. They are not in use anywhere in the world today except by aboriginal tribes mostly in pursuit of wild game and by uncivilized tribes who believe brutality is the only means to an end.

Though Khan's way appeared integrated, it was not inclusive and didn't allow for individual creativeness so his people never got any better than Khan's knowledge allowed them to be. This is true of many bureaucratic organizations today as well. Even though the old methods no longer work, many of today's leaders still have the Khan mindset and are still using fear and shame to control their people. As was the case with the Mongol armies, these methods are doomed to fail. What toppled the Mongol empire was new knowledge and new awareness. The same thing will bring down the great corporate giants who continue to follow this model.

It is inevitable that as collective knowledge expands, the power of knowledge in the hands of a few will decline. Faster, more nimble "armies" are emerging and old-line, single-focused loyalties are being quickly replaced by innovative thinking, global awareness, long-term focus, and more meaningful work. Knowledge truly is power and power cannot remain in the hands of a few in an information age where knowledge is readily available to the masses.

People dead-set on living true to their values will always be an immovable force. The newer generations are deeply and broadly informed. They have a much broader and more inclusive view. They believe they have a right to make choices, to be heard and valued, to contribute in a meaningful way, to be respected and consulted. In short, to be happy and fulfilled in their work. They know how to use the knowledge available to them for leverage and they use it regularly. The worldview of Generation X and Millennials has given them a whole different view of leadership and prevents them from even considering that the old model of one great leader might have any value. The model, therefore, even when modified for a more civil world, has little power.

A very wide gap exists between the emerging workforce and typical organizations and it is getting wider. To bridge it, leaders need to understand, from a macro level to a micro one, why the gap exists. From a macro level, an awareness of global memes, which are ideas, behaviors and beliefs that spread within a culture and become a part of the collective mind, can aid in understanding the gap that exists between established organizations and the incoming workforce. With understanding, adjustments can be made to begin bridging it.

The model of social dynamics described by researcher and author, Dr. Don Beck, in his book, *Spiral Dynamics* is an excellent model for exploring how gaps occur on a macro level. Though populations exist on varying levels and can shift from one meme to another based on circumstances and associations, individuals, groups and organizations tend to function from particular levels in particular settings. For example, some individuals tend to hold to one meme personally, another religiously and still another in business.

Organizations move much slower than individuals and tend to continue holding to a particular level that has worked for them long after the general population has progressed to other levels. Gaps occur when the meme that defines a generation is too far removed from the organizational meme.

Once individuals have gained new awareness and new abilities, they don't go backwards except for a particular reason and then only briefly. The collective mind does not contract, it continues to expand. Organizations, governing bodies and tribes that have experienced success using a particular system, continue to cling to that system. But the continued evolution of collective awareness creates a gap which continues to widen until the entrenched, slow to change bodies are forced to adjust.

Most long established organizations are still functioning on levels 3 through 5 of Beck's model (illustration 2.1) while the general population has continued to evolve. Traditionalists functioned within that range so there was not a lot of pushback from that generation. Baby Boomers had evolved to level 6 and began to resist established organizations, though not radically. The values and mindset of Generation X moved to level 7 and Millennials have moved to level 8, which is at least three evolutions removed from the level on which established organizations function.

Spiral Dynamics Meme Levels

9	**Aspirational** (Spiral Dynamics Coral) Wisdom-focused, driven to explore limits of human capacity
8	**Holistic** (Spiral Dynamics Turquoise) Systemic, experiential, driven by desire for unity & meaning
7	**Integrative** (Spiral Dynamics Yellow) Interdependent, flexible, accepting, driven by functionality
6	**Affiliative** (Spiral Dynamics Green) Seeks connectivity and meaning, driven by human rights
5	**Pragmatist** (Spiral Dynamics Orange) Materialistic, self-reliant, driven by desire to get ahead
4	**Absolutist** (Spiral Dynamics Blue) Obedient to higher authority, driven by fear of punishment
3	**Egocentric** (Spiral Dynamics Red) Aggressive, exploitative, driven by power and conquest
2	**Indigenous** (Spiral Dynamics Purple) Tribal, ritualistic, driven by belief in mysterious powers
1	**Archaic** (Spiral Dynamics Beige) Instinctive, survival-focused, driven by biological urges

Adapted from Don Beck's Spiral Dynamics Model

Illustration 2.1

In that humanity as a whole does not devolve, the gap that exists between most organizations and Millennials must be bridged. To get the most from this generation, organizational leaders will need to evolve too

Organizations still stuck on the levels of power and conquest (3), authority and rules (4), and get ahead at all costs (5) will need to become more holistic and collaborative in their approach to reach Millennials. This generation does not now, and never will, tolerate egocentric behaviors and they are quick to abandon organizations and systems where hierarchies exist. Their willingness to walk away puts the power in their hands and places the onus for building that bridge squarely on the shoulders of organizational leaders.

If It Isn't Working…

Many people question why the old model is still in use at all when it is producing more effort than ease. In our experience, the two primary reasons are fear and lack of awareness. When it's fear, it's usually fear of upsetting the status quo, losing time, money, respect or some other valuable resource, or of repercussions from the old-school leaders. Potentially progressive leaders who have been sold on the idea that the old model is "tried, true and proven" don't want to risk stepping into new territory even if what they are doing is not working.

Leaders who want to build a strong, healthy organization don't need to start from an unknown. Although rare, there are effective organizational models with highly effective leaders who continue to prove the power and profitability of that new model. This new model is as tried and true as the old. More importantly, it works exceptionally well now, and will far into the future.

CHAPTER THREE
Lessons from a Maverick

"We could have high performance teams if people would just do what their leaders tell them to," announced one corporate manager during a needs assessment interview. This is an all too common sentiment in many corporations. Leaders keep pushing for performance and teamwork, and keep thinking the problem is the people they employ. They keep adding perks, providing training and more training, and going through all the prescribed motions, but few are actually getting the results they hope for. On the surface it appears there are lots of reasons why. In reality, there is only one: a flawed leadership model.

It's easy to look at under-performing employees and assume there is something inherently wrong with *them* or to assume that systems need updating. It is not so easy to look at the core tenets of an organization and consider that the problem might stem from there. Yet, in all the years we have worked with organizations, where there are systemic problems in established businesses, the source can always be traced back to the leadership model. There three primary factors affecting performance in the workplace . They are:

1. Leadership

2. Environment

3. Job Fit

Ultimately, environment and job fit boil down to leadership because leaders determine the environment and how effectively the organization recruits, hires, places and promotes its people. They determine who stays and who leaves, and under what conditions.

If every person and team were truly empowered to perform to capacity, then every organization would hum like a healthy beehive. Empowered employees are fully engaged in their work, both mentally and emotionally, and they are fully invested in the company for which they work. Leaders of highly functional organizations foster an environment where employees develop and grow on every level, and they frequently make a radical departure from business as usual.

One example is Brazilian businessman, Ricardo Semler, who by dumping his family business' old model and adopting an entirely new one, turned the aging Semco Corporation into one of the most revolutionary business success stories of our time. One of his first acts was to eliminate unnecessary layers of management and allow employees true democracy in the workplace. This revolutionary shift created a company that blazed a path to unprecedented success even in the midst of an uncertain economy. Semler's leadership style and innovative business management policies led to such increased innovation and employee engagement that company revenue leapt from $4 million in 1982 to $212 million in 2004. Semler's unorthodox leadership style was the subject of his popular book, *Maverick: The Success Story Behind the World's Most Unusual Workplace,* and it continues to attract interest around the world (Semler 1995).

Semler's first consideration in an employee is not skills, but what he calls character. He explains his employment philosophy by quoting the parable of three stone cutters. When each was asked what they did, the first stone cutter described himself as "a man who cuts stones." The second described himself as "a craftsman who painstakingly cuts stones into specific shapes." The third described himself as "an artist who builds cathedrals." It is this third type of employee Semler says he seeks. And, having found this type, he gives them the respect they deserve, the structure to thrive in, and the freedom to shine. "Freedom," Semler says, "is a prime driver for performance." We agree. It's a prime driver for every generation and particularly for Gen Xers and Millennials, which studies suggest will occupy 75% of the workforce by 2025.

At Semco Partners, employees are free to do such unconventional things as interview and select their own bosses, and fire them if they don't measure up. They can decide whether or not a scheduled meeting is important enough to attend and can choose not to attend if they see no value in it. They have the choice to work flexible hours and from home where possible, and have had this flexibility since 1981. More than twenty years later very few organizations have adopted this practice. Most leaders cringe when Semler's model is even suggested as an option. They can't imagine a workplace so "loosely" run and yet this is precisely the workplace organizations will need to embrace in order to get the best from the incoming workforce.

When asked if he thought his maverick style would work in any organization, Semler replied, "This is an exercise in sociology and anthropology and has to do with respecting tribes. It has very little to do with the types of companies. So, yes, it seems universally applicable to all people and how they work. We've seen that proved in practice by police divisions, hospitals and schools in many parts of the globe, and in many different types of organizations that have seen our way of doing things and have implemented similar concepts."

Before it can work in other organizations, leaders must be willing to relinquish the kind of control they have become accustomed to and adopt a more collaborative mindset. Most leaders strongly resist even the idea of collaboration versus control. What they don't yet see is that their need to retain control is exactly what will cause them to *lose* control as the new generations populate the workplace. Leaders who cannot let go of the old ways will become effete and irrelevant and, at that point, they will have no choice but to relinquish control.

Ultimately, it all boils down to control. A reporter from *Ode Magazine* asked Semler why so few companies in the world run like Semco. Semler speculated that it was because managers are afraid to lose power and control. There is a lot of evidence to support that hypothesis. Many leaders fear that giving their employees the kind of freedom Semler describes would foster an environment where slackers would reign, but studies suggest otherwise. Where the right people with the right mindset are selected in the first place and placed in the right jobs, they take responsibility for themselves and for seeing to it that the company is thriving. In such an environment the system naturally self-corrects.

Wise leaders realize they can best maintain control by making that inevitable shift before it becomes necessary. It's the only way to ensure that change is measured, healthy, and beneficial, and everyone comes away a winner.

In the new model, the leader's focus is on managing and maintaining the *environment* rather than the people. Studies show that, when the environment supports high performance, those who don't fit become uncomfortable enough to either correct their behaviors so they fit in or they leave. The trick is to discover what attributes and characteristics work best in your particular organization.

To get there, many leaders will have to change their assumptions and mindset around leadership. Most leaders are familiar with Douglas McGregor's Theory X and Theory Y management models. Neither model has been effective at producing the desired effect. Fewer leaders are familiar with the Theory Z model, but they should be. It's the model highly successful organizations are using. The Theory Z model was first suggested by psycholgist, Dr. Abraham Maslow, as a factor for optimal performance where work adds to one's perception of meaning and significance. We redefined it for the world of business after years of studying employee motivation and performance factors and observing that in most cases neither Theory X nor Theory Y management practices led to high performance workforces. Let's examine all three models.

Theory X assumes that the average human being is lazy and self-centered, lacks ambition, dislikes change, and needs to be told what to do. The corresponding managerial approach emphasizes total control and suggests that employees are motivated through fear, pain and carefully meted out rewards for good behavior. The problem with this model is that it has never worked to motivate people to higher performance. In fact, it has just the opposite effect, yet it is still the most frequently used.

Theory Y maintains that human beings are active rather than passive shapers of themselves and of their environment. They long to grow and assume responsibility and, given the chance, will do that. The managerial approach in this instance is to manage as little as possible. The approach here is "give them plenty of sunshine and water, and let them grow and blossom." This theory asserts that people are inherently self-starting and self-organizing and will achieve miracles if given the chance. The problem with this model is that it paints a picture that often leads to laissez-faire management where people are managed too loosely and a no-consequence culture develops.

Theory Z combines the best of X and Y and moves management to true leadership levels. Theory Z maintains that people need both the freedom to make decisions and shape their world *and* the structure to make the most of their innate tendencies and capacities. Though all people have innate skills, abilities and drivers, not all have developed them well. Individuals are effective only to the degree they have developed their inate skills and abilities. For most people, both tight controls and too much freedom result in high frustration and fear, not in high performance. Theory Z asserts (and has a lot of research to validate) that people perform best in an environment where they have a structured foundation and clear boundaries that support their natural inclinations, and which provide a lot of freedom to function and perform within that structure. Employees of Theory X managers can only grow to the level the manager allows. Employees of Theory Y managers can only grow to the level their current development allows. Employees of Theory Z leaders can grow to their highest potential.

Attribute	Theory X	Theory Y	Theory Z
Motivation	External Must Be Motivated	Internal Self-motivated	Internal, but Needs a Catalyst
Responsibility	People Avoid It	People Enjoy It	People Enjoy It Once Developed
Management	Authoritarian	Laissez-Faire	Participative
Decisions	Management	Collaborative	Collaborative
Control	Centralized	Decentralized	Defined and Distributed
Delegation	Tasks	Projects	Projects and Performance
Direction	Strict Rules	Unstructured	Structured Freedom
Delivery	Force Performance	Inspire Performance	Inspire & Guide Performance
Skills	Repetitive Work	Specialized Work	Individualized Work
Change	People Resist It	People Adapt To It	People Grow Through It
Training	Random – Task Improvement	Random – Pers. Development	Targeted – Cont. Improvement
Rewards	Determined by Performance (P)	Determined by Values (V)	Determined by P and V

Illustration 3.1

Copyright Sherry D. Buffington 2013

Semler's people are an example of the effect of Theory Z. They have grown way beyond his personal capacity and he loves it. He has applied the Theory Z model of leadership brilliantly providing both structure and freedom, and his people have responded brilliantly. Semler says he is regularly surprised by the heights his people reach. He loves their contributions and his people love the faith he keeps showing in them. Like most of the great leaders we have studied, Semler chooses good people, expects the best from them, regularly conveys both his expectations and his belief in his people, and then sets them free to perform.

7 Things Theory Z Leaders Do to Keep Employees Performing at Peak Capacity and Loving It:

1. **Regularly and consistently convey the company's purpose and mission** as well as the leader's vision so employees know the importance of their job, and the value the company brings to the community and the world.

2. **Remain accessible to employees** - listen to their suggestions - value their input - show them they are relevant. The more accessible leaders are to their people, the higher are trust and engagement levels. Theory Z leaders make sure they stay closely connected to their employees on every level.

3. **Take steps to be certain each employee is in the right job and feels the work they are doing is meaningful.** In his book, *The Soul of the Organization: How to Ignite Employee Engagement and Productivity at Every Level*, David B. Zenoff observes, "Middle income Americans often experience the most stress from feeling they are wasting their lives doing meaningless work. They hunger to serve the common good and to contribute something with their talents and energies, yet find that their actual work gives them little opportunity to do so." (December 2012, Apress) This is especially true of Millennials who highly value meaningful work. As the power shift occurs and Millennials dominate the workplace, companies that fail to convey meaning to their workers will struggle to keep employees on the job, much less engaged and productive.

4. **Provide flexibility.** Women have long been willing to leave an organization to create the flexible life they desire. Today younger professional men are doing the same thing because they have a different view of ambition and different ideas about the importance of life/work balance and family. Among Millennials neither males nor females tolerate long hours or rigid schedules and they tend to leave employers that are unwilling to allow time for personal and family life. Generally, the ones who leave most readily are the brightest and most talented.

5. **Make sure the salaries of the highest paid are not too far above the average pay scale.** Studies show that motivation begins to drop off in direct proportion to the disparity between the pay of C level executives and the average worker. The greater the disparity, the greater the level of disengagement. The reasoning of companies that pay exorbitant CEO salaries is that they must match the salaries made public to attract top talent. What they fail to see is that top talent can't make a company successful when its employees are disengaged, and one reason they are disengaged is because of the wide gap between employee salaries and the exorbitant salaries of leaders.

An article in *Huffington Post* (10/28/13) points to the toxic effect of overblown salaries for CEOs giving the example of JC Penney's former CEO, Ronald Johnson. Johnson worked for JC Penney for 18 months and received 53.3 million dollars when he left even though, during his tenure, the company had a 25% drop in sales and wasted millions more following a formula doomed to fail.

Most research suggests that a ratio larger than 10:1 leads to employee resentment and disengagement, but most organizations are not open to narrowing the income disparity to anywhere near that level. That's unfortunate, because companies are losing billions of dollars in productivity as a result. And it gets worse.

According to a study done through Vanderbilt University by Dr. William H. Anderson, higher salaries actually *inversely* correlate to values such as honesty, trust, respect, commitment, discipline, sharing and forgiving. In other words, *the higher the salary, the lower these values rank* (*illustration 3.2*).

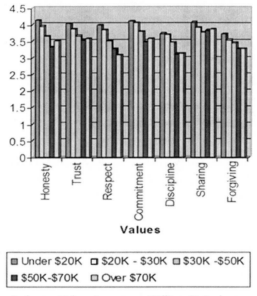

LS Mean Value Scores by Salary Level

Anderson Values Inventory, William H. Anderson

Illustration 3.2

Millennials are not as money driven as employees in the past have been. They are more interested in learning and growing in ways that are significant to them and their future, so there may be a way to bridge the salary gap in the future that will not necessarily mean greatly reducing the salaries of CEOs or greatly increasing the salaries of employees. For Millennials, the wage disparity will only be a problem if the leader is not contributing sufficiently to warrant the wage level. Though it's hard to imagine that employees would consider the contributions of any individual to be thousands of times more valuable than those of the average person, it could happen. Star performers and athletes make thousands more than the average performer or athlete and their fans don't seem to have a problem with that.

6. **Remain transparent.** Employees need to know what leaders expect, what the company is doing at any given time, what changes are occurring, or are about to occur, where the changes are leading, as well as salaries and job descriptions companywide. When leaders are not willing to disclose the facts, employees assume the company has something to hide and tend not to trust the company or its leaders. Trust is directly correlated to engagement.

7. **Give employees choices.** Policies and procedures manuals only go so far. Theory Z leaders make sure managers and workers make decisions together when possible and keep one another informed otherwise. Decisions are not left up to the Board of Directors or CEO. They purposefully strip away blind authoritarianism which leads to greater engagement and increased productivity, and give workers the tools and structure they need to self-govern and self-manage. Not only are workers more engaged and productive when they are given healthy structure within which they can self-govern, self-governing employees also make their managers' job so much easier.

The key to successful leadership today is influence, not authority.

Ken Blanchard

Progress occurs when courageous, skillful leaders seize the opportunity to change things for the better.

Harry S Truman

CHAPTER FOUR
Game Changers

For generations, the core values people held made managing them relatively easy. The Traditional generation, and every generation before them, learned the values of obedience, hard work, and self-sacrifice. These served an agrarian society and the industrial world quite well. No one questioned authority, or even thought to question it, until a few bold souls stepped outside the box and had the audacity to do so. Unions were born as a result.

Power shifts occur when generational values depart dramatically from those of previous generations. Significant shifts began toward the end of the traditional era as information became more readily available and have grown larger with each new generation. Not every person in each generation follows the trend, of course, but the overall trend sets the standard for generations and affects societies, marketplaces, and businesses for years to come. The first union was formed in the United States in 1866. It took another hundred years for the first power shift to occur. The next two

The First Power Shift - From Authoritarian Control to Personal Power

The new mindset introduced by union creators was readily picked up by other groups and reported on by the media, which gave Baby Boomers access to out-of-the-box thinking. They had access to the personal rights philosophies of union organizers and civil rights leaders early in life and they bought into that philosophy, which introduced the first major shift from authoritarian control to personal power as baby boomers began to move into the workplace around 1966.

Boomers had Traditional parents who instilled in them the values of obedience and hard work, but they rejected the self-sacrifice value. To accommodate the shift in values, organizations began to smooth the rough edges of the authoritarian model that then ruled the workplace and to take a more people-friendly approach. They added perks like cafeterias with healthy food selections and workout rooms in campus-like settings. Some even added onsite daycare centers. These accommodations were sufficient for the Baby Boom generation and leaders went back to business as usual thinking everything had been handled. And it had been, until Generation X entered the workplace.

The Second Power Shift - Personal Power to Disempowered

The values of Generation X departed even farther from traditional values, creating yet another power shift. Baby Boomers were the primary influencers of this shift. As parents, Boomers taught their children to value personal power and independent thinking, but they didn't push the values of obedience and hard work onto their children as their Traditional parents had on them. The perception of Boomers was that obedience and hard work limited personal power and this was among the highest of their values.

Generation X brought the second power shift into the workplace when they began entering it around 1986. This one was an even greater departure from corporate values and left many leaders baffled as to how to manage this generation.

Baby Boomers had parents who went through the great depression and who were overly cautious and conservative as a result. Baby Boomers en masse decided they would not treat their children or other people in the strict and restrictive ways they were treated so the pendulum swung to the other extreme and a laissez faire approach was the result. Baby Boomers are notorious for their laissez faire management and parenting styles. They saw this hands-off approach as a way to promote, or at least allow, freedom and personal power. This created a big problem because centuries of close management had not prepared employees to manage themselves. The result has been a sort of helter-skelter environment where employees are not sure what to do and react by becoming overly cautious and often disengage.

The result of this was that managers (and parents) regularly got poor results which increased stress levels and created situations where Boomers defaulted to the old Traditional models, which they didn't manage well. Under stress laissez faire managers look very much like authoritarian managers who push for results. Add lack of structure and what you get is micro-managers. The drastic shifts between the hands-off "do what you think is right" approach to the strict "do as I say" approach creates a great deal of confusion and frustration. This lack of consistency is one factor feeding the high percentage of disengaged employees which polls reveal year after year. Between 2000 and 2014 engagement levels have remained pretty much the same according to *Gallup* polls. Approximately 73% of the workforce remains disengaged.

Though the intent of Boomers was to provide freedom and personal power, without clear boundaries and the structure to support these, the result was chaos and high stress rather than the effectiveness that was intended. The unstructured laissez faire approach to parenting and leadership resulted in a generation that saw no clear future and decided the best survival strategy was to simply disengage. This shifted the power from the individual to no one and, where no one has legitimate power, forced power becomes necessary. That never works though, especially with people who are already disengaged.

Row, Row, Row Your Boat

Imagine your business as a rowing crew with 10 people rowing and one directing the crew. On a rowing team the director is called the coxswain. Though the coxswain does not row, this position is just as essential as that of each rower. The coxswain's primary job is to keep the boat moving forward in a straight line. In addition to steering the boat, the coxswain helps the crew keep the cadence by calling out instructions and the stroke rate. If the boat can't stay in its lane, it gets disqualified so keeping it on course is critical to success. Coxswains steer the boat by making minor corrections in the direction of the rudder and making sure all rowers are equally engaged. They manage its speed by motivating the team. The coxswain is responsible for the safety of all the rowers in the boat and of the equipment. Sounds a lot like the duties of company leaders, doesn't it?

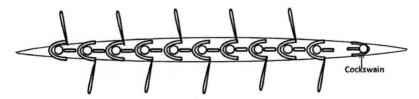

Cockswain

Coxswains control the team by using a "cox-box" which provides the current stroke rate much like the metrics organizations use to measure the effectiveness of their people. If the stroke rate is off-pace, they will instruct the "stroke" to control the rate and bring it back to race pace. The stroke is the most important position in the boat because the stroke rower sets the stroke rate and rhythm for the rest of the crew to follow.

Now imagine that the rower sitting next to the stroke is disengaged and not rowing at all. Further imagine that five of the ten rowers are barely rowing and another one is purposefully rowing backwards. Imagine the challenges the three effective rowers would have trying to row around the seven who were actively disengaged or under-performing. Imagine the stress levels of the coxswain as he tried one thing after another to get the team working together without success.

When all of the rowers are exhausted (or in this case the three that are rowing), they depend on the coxswain for motivation and the determination to win; to add that extra bit of strength they need to keep going. A coxswain must be more than just a good communicator; he must stay calm during the whole race and sound confident. But, if most of the team was under-performing, how calm or confident do you suppose he would remain?

This scenario is what is happening in companies everywhere because overall 50% of employees are disengaged (not rowing very hard), 20% are *actively* disengaged (purposefully rowing backwards or not at all) and only 30% are engaged (rowing well). Is it any wonder stress levels are so high?

In the rowing example, rowers help the coxswain by being attentive and keeping their focus on what's happening in the boat. They can't see where the boat is headed and need to trust their leader to tell them where the other boats are positioned. On the rare occasion when the coxswain finds his boat in a dangerous position, he needs to know that the crew trusts him and will respond to his calls immediately.

Even with the proper intention, when the team falters and the leader loses his cool, resistance comes up and the trust and confidence of the team drops. As this occurs, the rhythm of the team goes off and both speed and precision are compromised. This can be readily seen in a rowing team because a race moves quickly and if synchronization is not immediately recovered, the race is lost.

In organizations, even if leaders intend to lead effectively, as most do, but lose their cool because their team is disengaged and not working together, stress is what rules the day both for the leader and the team. And where stress rules, the thinking brain disengages and the reactionary brain takes over. So, in time, the effectiveness of the leader and of those they are trying to lead becomes seriously compromised. Although the consequences are not as immediately apparent in a company as they are in a boat race, they are just as damaging in the long run.

The Third Power Shift - Disempowered to Global Power

The third and most dramatic shift started around 2003 when Millennials began entering the workplace. The values of this generation are an even further departure from the standard corporate model. They abhor hierarchies and are intolerant of organizations where they exist.

Where organizations value profit and position, Millennials value collaboration, work-life balance, and making a significant difference in the world, and they can't see working for, or even supporting, organizations which lack these values.

Because they grew up with the internet, Millennials have a global view which has given them a sense of power no generation before them has ever had. They feel connected to the whole world. They see the suffering in Africa, the turmoil in the Mideast, the demonstrations in the streets of Egypt, the inefficiencies of governments, the effect of corporate greed and the corporations that are guilty of it.

They also see opportunities on a global scale and can compare organizations around the world, which makes competing for top talent and maintaining their loyalties a much greater challenge. From their global view, Millennials can see what's wrong and what needs to be done to make things better on a broader scale and they are willing to stand up for what's right on a broader scale. They don't typically choose to fight, but they do take action. When they see injustice, unfairness or lack of cooperation, they simply walk away figuratively (mentally or emotionally disengage) or literally (physically walk out the door). We are more than ten years into this cycle which is projected to last at least forty more years, with deepening idealistic values continuing to increase over time.

Idealism Versus Core Values

Millennials are often disparaged as idealists who expect the world to be handed to them on a platter. An article in *Huffington Post (September 2013)*, which reflects what we often hear from managers, states; "To be clear, Gen Y (Millennials) want economic prosperity just like their parents did. They also want to be fulfilled by their career in a way their parents didn't think about as much. The career goals of Gen Y as a whole have become much more particular and ambitious, but they have been given a second message throughout their childhood as well: *you're special!* This generation has been taught, 'everyone will go and get themselves some fulfilling career, but *I am unusually wonderful* and as such, my career and life path will stand out amongst the crowd.' So on top of the generation as a whole having the bold goal of a flowery career, *each individual* thinks that *he* or *she* is destined for something even better."

Every generation is idealistic in their youth. Idealism wanes as we age, but core values remain constant. There is a big difference between the idealism of youth and core values, and it is *core values*, not idealism that drives power shifts. In 2015 the majority of Millennials are still in their twenties and younger so, of course, they are idealistic. So were Traditionalists, Baby Boomers and Gen Xers when they were young. Boomers were the original flower children who were determined to affect world peace. They were the hippies who preached "make love not war." They elevated the peace symbol to a worldwide brand. Those ideals changed as they matured, but their core values of personal power and freedom never did. Those core values are what caused the shift in the way companies currently do business. The same will hold true of Millennials. So, if you have been thinking they will someday grow up and look like Traditionals, think again.

Millennials catch a lot of flak; some of it valid—most of it ill-informed. Too often critics unfairly condemn a generation that wasn't exactly dealt the best hand when it came to the world they inherited and who are still quite young and idealistic. Actually, Millennials have a lot to be proud of. They are civic minded, genuinely concerned about other people and want to do something meaningful. They are better educated, more aware, more technically savvy, better at strategic thinking and better prepared to navigate the fast-paced, attention-deficit world we have created. They have a lot of really powerful attributes that leaders would be wise to acknowledge and tap into.

The cover of the May 2013 issue of Time Magazine proclaimed Millennials to be the "Me Me Me" Generation. That's a terrible mischaracterization. The more mature Millennials are anything but selfish and me-focused. According to a Huffington Post article (June 2012), three-fourths of Millennials ages 20 to 35 responding to an online survey said they had donated money to charity in the year the survey was conducted and 63 percent said they'd spent time volunteering. Me-focused people are not inclined to do that.

More Insights into Millennials

Millennials are Civic Minded

- Millennials donate time or money to organizations they have researched to ensure the organization is doing something useful.
- Volunteer applications have increased significantly since the 1990s and continue to increase.
- Millennials are considered the most civic-minded generation since those born in the 1930s and 1940s.

Millennials are Better Educated

- Millennials are the most educated generation in history according to a 2012 *Pew Research Center* report.
- Millennials are willing to make sacrifices in pursuit of education and most say they want to learn something new when they travel. Almost all state that they expect continual learning in the workplace.

Meaningful Work Matters

- Millennials say their most important priority is to be a good parent and raise responsible, well-adjusted children. The next highest priority is having a successful marriage followed by helping others in need.

- They are focused on meaningful work. Having a high-paying career or fame is low on the priority list for this generation.
- 67% of Millennials define success as "being smart and well-read."
- 84% say making a difference in the world is more important than professional recognition.
- 92% believe businesses should be measured by more than their profits.
- A greater proportion of Millennials do not identify with any particular religion, though most believe "God exists" and value prayer as much as previous generations.
- 72 % say they are "more spiritual than religious." (Charitable Giving Study 2013)

Learning and Personal Growth are More Important than Money

- Millennials actively look for ways to improve their outcomes and are keenly aware of the importance of continual learning. They report that they will stay with a company as long as they are learning and growing and are quick to leave when they feel there is nothing else to learn.
- Learning to Millennials extends far beyond job-based learning. They want their learning to be relevant to effective living and personal success as well as to job performance.

When Will They Act Like Us?

We recently worked with 45 key managers of a large one hundred year old multinational consumer products company. We did a two-day session that focused on helping these managers move from an authoritarian management mindset to one of a more inclusive, coaching approach. During our pre-work and curriculum development, the decision committee told us they wanted us to devote several hours to review how generational differences could be understood and leveraged through our coaching model. We built that into the two-day agenda. Then, upon arrival the day before the program, we were told to cut the generational review portion of the program. When we asked why, one of the decision-makers explained that most of the managers attending the program had recently been through a generational diversity session and the committee had decided they didn't want to "overdo it."

Marc pointed out that 95% of the managers in the room were Baby Boomers who had indicated in a survey that generational differences was an area they did not understand and a primary source of frustration. The survey had also revealed a rather alarming statistic that the decision-makers didn't seem too concerned with. Over 60% of survey respondents indicated they would *leave the company* if they could. Despite the strong evidence that managers wanted and needed greater awareness in the area of generational differences and strong indications that better understanding among managers was needed, the generational session was scuttled.

Throughout the training, questions about generational differences arose and each time one of the Boomer managers would share a story of how frustrated they were with trying to manage Gen Xers or Millennials.

Though that part of the training had been eliminated, participants returned to the subject time and time again and it was clear that more indepth learning in this area would be necessary for the company to keep their younger workforce interested and motivated to perform. Several managers ended their tale of woe with some version of "when will they start acting more like us?"

Our answer was, and always is, "*never!*" Every generation has shaped the world in its own image and that will never change. Baby Boomers, who are now so intent on changing Gen Xers and Millennials, were themselves instruments of dramatic change in the workplace. Baby Boomers didn't give up their beliefs or cultural strategies to appease their parents or their employers and neither will Generation X or Millennials. Companies had to adjust to fit Baby Boomer requirements then and they will have to adjust now. Only now, the adjustment will need to be a huge departure from what organizations have used for hundreds of years and come to rely on. The idealism of youth changes and matures over time, but core values never change.

The reason organizations provide cafeterias filled with healthy food choices, on-site exercise facilities, child-care facilities and all sorts of other amenities today is because Baby Boomers insisted upon them. Traditionals never got or expected those things. Baby Boomers did and companies had to adjust.

Other, even more dramatic adjustments will have to occur as Millennials, a cohort that is 80 million strong and even larger than the Baby Boom generation, populates the workplace. The benefit of making those adjustments can be seen by looking at the meteoric growth of Gen X and Millennial driven companies like Google, Facebook, Zappos, and progressive companies like Costco which have created a culture that serves the needs and values of the newer generations.

This massive third shift has begun and it will inevitably continue. Leaders who recognize this fact and begin adjusting now will be able to ride it out and perhaps even take their organization to great new heights as the new model organizations have done. The changes needed to keep Millennials engaged are not an option, they are a necessity. True leaders will step up to the challenge, learn what they need to do, and make the changes. Who these true leaders are will become apparent in the next ten to twelve years as the new model companies grow and thrive while those that cling to the old model struggle to survive.

> *No generation will reshape itself and its values to accommodate another generation. It has never happened and it never will. The sooner leaders and managers grasp this fact, the sooner they can begin making the necessary adjustments to get the best from their people and catapult themselves and their company to new levels of effectiveness.*

CHAPTER FIVE
Getting the Best from People

When we ask managers what they most want, the primary answer is some form of "I want high performing people who are committed to doing a good job." That answer keeps coming up because the strategies and methods leaders and managers have been trying are not working well and, generally, they have no idea why.

Getting the best from people is both a science and an art. The science is in knowing how to uncover the essential factors for motivation and combine them in just the right way to get to the gold. The art is in actually doing it.

The goal of motivation is to direct behaviors toward a particular outcome. The problem is that most people focus on behaviors when they are trying to motivate others rather than on the reason for the behaviors. When the reasons change, the behaviors change. To get to the reasons, however, requires a much deeper view than most managers have or think they need.

Most managers have been taught to manage at a surface level. They have been told that if they provide enough strokes and incentives, and balance them out with enough consequences, people will behave as expected. In the short term such tactics work often enough to keep getting repeated, but these are extrinsic motivators and are temporary at best. For extrinsic motivation to continue to produce results, the ante has to be continually increased which, over time, gets very expensive and time-consuming. Besides the cost in time and money, extrinsic or externally applied incentives and consequences are only marginally effective and they quickly lose their effect. That's why managers spend so much time looking for new and better incentives, or imposing harsher penalties. At some point the ante cannot reasonably get any larger or the punishment more severe and, at that point, "motivation" ends and disengagement begins.

All *real* motivation is *intrinsic* and, unless leaders and managers understand what leads to intrinsic motivation and how to activate it, they will continue to search fruitlessly for ways to keep their people motivated. Intrinsic motivation is self-perpetuating. It feeds desires and brings out the genius and star power in people. We believe that almost everyone has at least one area of genius; at least one place where they can really shine. Not many have developed their natural skills and abilities to that point, but they can be developed in almost everyone. True genius is an ideal combination of inherent traits and abilities optimally enhanced by the effective development of complementary skills.

It was once believed that if an individual didn't already have natural traits and abilities developed by adulthood, it is too late to develop them. The ability to observe living brains using functional magnetic resonance imaging (FMRI) has shown just the opposite. A new science called neuroplasticity has proven the capacity of humans to learn and relearn throughout life. It has also shown that learning takes place best when the motivation centers are active.

On the other side of the equation, the ability to observe living brains has led to the startling discovery that learning, and even emotional control, declines when people are exposed to stressful situations. In a study published in *Biological Psychiatry* Yale researchers reported that stress actually *reduces* gray matter in critical regions of the brain that regulate emotion and important physiological functions even in healthy individuals. Prolonged stress has been linked to changes in brain structure which result in depression, anxiety, illness and even addictions. (Yale News, 2012)

Poor performance and disengagement in the workplace is almost always the result of leaders or managers failing to discover and tap into intrinsic motivators. The practice of firing under-performers without first trying to engage them at an intrinsic level is a big problem in more ways than one. It's a very costly practice that rarely yields good results. In fact, when people are routinely fired and replaced, stress goes up for the remaining employees, and morale, motivation, and performance tends to drop off. Employees can push past stressors only so long and then something has got to give. What generally "gives" is the drive to perform.

Three Levels of Intrinsic Motivation

There are three levels on which people can be intrinsically motivated and all three can yield powerful results, but to activate them requires a deeper level of awareness than most managers take the time to develop.

The three levels are:

- Basic human needs
- Generationally-based core values
- Personality-specific preferences and needs

The three levels are shown in *illustration 5.1.*

Illustration 5.1

Basic Motivators

The broadest and the easiest level to tap into is the level of basic needs. To motivate on this level, all we need to know is the four primary or basic human needs and how to appeal to them. The four needs are easy to remember by using "BASE" as an acronym. They are:

Belonging

Acceptance

Significance

Ego gratification (satisfaction/happiness)

Although these are the easiest to tap into, they will only take you so far. The base motivation level informs us that all people seek belonging, acceptance, significance and ego gratification in the form of personal satisfaction and happiness, but it doesn't tell us *how* those basic needs look from generation to generation or from person to person. What feels like belonging to one person, for example, might be very different to another. To be truly influential, you will need to look deeper.

Generational Motivators (Core Values)

The next level in is core values which are broad-based beliefs that are specific to particular generations or cohorts. Though cultural differences alter generational values to some degree, They are surprisingly similar from culture to culture.

To tap into these motivators, it is necessary to understand the generation an individual identifies with as well as the culture they grew up in. Discerning generational affiliation isn't as simple as knowing an individual's birth year or approximate age. It's a mistake to assume that an individual identifies with the generation of people who fall into their age group. This is especially true of people born at the beginning or end of a generation. Early Baby Boomers may identify with Traditionalists, for example, while those born at the end of the Baby Boom era may well identify with Generation X or even Millennials.

Core values are shaped by the world we experience as we are growing up and are influenced not only by social norms, but also by the culture and class of people we most identify with. Generally, we form our beliefs and opinions of who we are and what life is about by the age of ten and that view doesn't change much unless we experience an event which is significant and emotionally impactful enough to cause us to back up and re-evaluate already developed beliefs. We continue to add supporting values as we gain additional knowledge, but we only accept the ones that align with our already established core beliefs and values. The experiences that shape core values are generally local (family of origin, school, peer group, church, etc.), but can be shaped by all the things we are regularly exposed to growing up.

Traditionalists were most influenced by local and regional events because that's the relatively narrow world they were exposed to growing up. Baby Boomers had national and international reach and, therefore, greater awareness. Generation X had global reach and awareness as do Millennials, but Millennials have expanded global reach even further and have added global connectivity and instant access to knowledge. Their instant global reach is one of the reasons for the great power shift which is now emerging and will continue through the foreseeable future.

From a global view, the wants and needs of a single organization looks puny and inconsequential, which gives Millennials a generally pessimistic view of organizations. They are impressed by integrity and adherence to a meaningful mission, not by an organization's size or marketing messages, which they can see right through. To keep the interest of Millennials, organizations have to convey a purpose much grander than just being an established and profitable enterprise. And, unless that grander purpose is consistently honored, keeping Gen Xers and Millennials engaged, or even on the job, will be a challenge.

To get the best from the new generations, and from every generation for that matter, leaders and managers need to understand on a much deeper level than most look, what makes them tick. *Illustration 5.2* provides a brief overview the values and expectation of every generation found in the workforce today.

	Traditionals 1922-1945	Baby Boomers 1946-1964	Generation X 1965-1980	Millennials 1981-2002
Work Ethic & Values	Work hard, respect authority, adhere to rules, duty first	Work efficiently, Question authority, Champion causes, seek personal fulfillment	Self-reliance, self-guidance, free to do the job and leave when done	Self-Reliance, entrepreneurial, independent contractor mindset
Work is Seen As	An obligation to be taken seriously	An arena for learning, growth and financial security	A negotiable contract which can be honored or broken	A means to an end, no more important than other aspects of life
Leadership Style	Follow directives, command and control	Consensual, laissez-faire	Equilateral, extends right to question and challenge	Collaborative, Personally and socially responsible
Motivators	Respect for experience and capabilities	Recognition, position, money, significance	Opportunity to contribute their way, flex time, few rules	Personally and socially meaningful work, and learning opportunities
Preferred Rewards	Security, money, benefits	Tangible rewards, promotions	Plenty of freedom and flexibility	Respect, participation in meaningful projects
Preferred Feedback	Acknowledgment of accomplishments	Acknowledgment of contribution/value	Fair and specific feedback on work	Information at the push of a button
Work & Family	Two different worlds, work must come first	Work to live, leaning toward work	Seeks to achieve work/life balance	Insists upon work/life balance

Illustration 5.2

© Copyright Sherry Buffington 2013

Although ideals and actions mature over time, short of having the rare significant emotional event, core *values stay the same* and are powerful motivators. Don't expect Generation X or Millennials to "grow up" and change their ways. If they are in the workforce, they have already grown up. You can certainly help them improve and polish their skills, but what will keep them motivated is already in place.

Personality Specific Motivators

Generational differences exist as a result of experiences common to an era and the values that form as a result. These values drive the major decisions of entire generations. Understanding generational values helps us manage people within cohorts more effectively, but to get the best from people, we have to meet them on a still deeper level because how people attend to the beliefs they hold depends on their individual personality.

Most leaders and managers don't bother to drill down as far as personality-based needs and that's a big mistake. When you can identify an individual's personality type and know the needs that lie behind that personality, you have the most powerful motivational tool on Earth. Everyone is seeking first and foremost to get their core needs met. These are *personal* needs which are specific to particular temperaments.

Unmet personal needs lead to stress, stress creates resistance, resistance lowers energy and interest, and lowered energy and interest kills motivation dead. The master key to motivation is the ability to reduce stress and satisfy needs. That is the essence of influence and those who have it are powerful leaders indeed. People will faithfully and without question follow a leader who makes their life better.

To gain the immense benefit of tapping into personality-based motivators (individual core needs) leaders need to know their people on this level. This may sound like a daunting task, but we have devised a method that makes discerning an individual's core personality quick and easy. With a little training, most people can correctly identify the personality and core needs of 90% to 95% of people just by observing them for a few minutes under certain conditions, which we teach our cleints to easily create.

There are four basic or core temperaments and each is motivated by a different set of needs. We use the *CORE Multidimensional Awareness*

Profile (CORE MAP) to define and describe the four types because it is a very in-depth assessment that accurately reflects far more than just observable or self-reported traits. It also reveals vitally important factors such as development levels across a broad range of behaviors, emotional intelligence in specific areas, how individuals are likely to act and react under varying levels of stress, task specific tolerance levels, and coping strategies. CORE is an acronym for Commander, Organizer, Relater and Entertainer. Most people have an image of what each of those look like which makes the names for each type easy to remember.

When you can identify an individual's core personality and know the needs that lie behind it, you know how to adjust your approach to get just the results you want.

Let's use as an example the broad-based value of integrity to show how personality-specific preferences influence the way that value is applied from one type to another.

The highest need for people who lead with Commander is to *get things done* so the value of integrity would play out for a Commander as making sure they get things done themselves and that those around them are doing the same.

For those who lead with Organizer, the highest need is to *get things right* so for them integrity would be making sure they were doing things right and seeing to it that others did the same.

For those who lead with Relater, the highest need is to *get along* with others. For them integrity would mean helping and supporting others, keeping things harmonic, and encouraging others to do the same.

For those who lead with Entertainer, the highest need is to *get connected* and to have first-hand experiences. For them integrity would mean connecting with people and life in a way that felt real and meaningful, and helping others do the same.

To learn more about CORE MAP and how you can use it to get a deeper, broader view of the people in your organization, scan the QR code, go to www. starperformancesystems.com and select the assesments tab.

The best way to gain the undying loyalty of others is to help them get their needs met. *Illustration 5.3* provides a list of the needs of the four CORE types. To be effective at using them, it is important to know how to read people non-verbally. Almost everyone tells the absolute truth about their naturally preferred style or combination of styles non-verbally, even if they are not consciously aware of their natural style. Unfortunately, few people know how to read those highly predictive non-verbal signals effectively so this great source of information goes largely untapped. This is one of the vitally important skills we teach leaders, managers and salespeople in our *Applied Intrinsic Motivation* (AIM) program. Clients rave about the results they get using this information and continue to reaffirm the value of tapping into core needs for motivating and positively influencing others.

The Four CORE Types and Related Needs

CORE Needs	
Commander • Action • Results • Accomplishment • Challenge • Efficiency • To appear competent • A sense of personal control • Primary need - Get it Done	**Entertainer** • A wide circle of influence • Appreciation (of self & accomplishments) • Open, visible recognition • Flexibility to explore and discover • First-hand experiences • Freedom from control and detail • To express self and be heard • Primary need - Get Connected
Organizer • Stability • Details and facts • Certainty • Order and logic • To be right or correct • Recognition for specific tasks • To perform a specific service • Primary need - Get it Right	**Relater** • Harmony or absence of conflict • Reassurance • Guidance and direction • Constancy and support • Security and stability • Flexibility for self and others • Consideration • Primary need - Get Along

Illustration 5.3

Motivating Behavioral Change

In truth, there are no *extrinsic* motivators, only extrinsic things that positively impact intrinsic motivators. Where there is no positive impact from an extrinsic effort, no motivation occurs. For example, if there is no intrinsic value placed on an award or trophy, receiving one may be seen as meaningless and actually act as a demotivator.

Long term behavioral change does not occur extrinsically either. As with motivators, for behavioral change to last, the reason for the change must be intrinsic. Negative behaviors are simply an external indicator that there is an internal issue that needs to be addressed. If we focus on the behavior, we miss the real issue. Here's how that looks:

- **Negative Behavior Occurs** – Negative behaviors are always a surface indicator of an issue that is producing stress.

- **Typical Reaction** – We judge the behavior, form an opinion, focus on the behavior, and try to induce a change in behavior through rewards or punishment.

- **Typical Effect** – Resistance, short-term change to the degree necessary; ineffective in the long term

- **More Effective Response** – (1) Notice the behavior, (2) find the *intent* behind the behavior, (3) find the *need* that drives the behavior, (4) discover the *value* that drives the need. Some needs are driven by the BASE motivators, some are driven by broad-based generational beliefs, and some are driven by personality-based needs.

Say, for example, that an employee who was once relatively timely begins showing up late on a regular basis. The typical response is to address the behavior, pointing out the obvious to the employee. "You have been late 8 times over the past three months and this has got to stop!" The result of this is resistance on the part of the employee. They may begin showing up on time to keep their job, but they are there in body only and, over time, the late behaviors are likely to return because the core issue has not been addressed.

A more effective response would be to discover and address the *reason* for the behavior. Though it isn't always obvious, behind every behavior there is a *positive* intent. Even bad behavior has a positive intent behind it. The intent is always to meet a need and, as mentioned earlier, the need can proceed from several sources; basic human needs, values-based needs or personality-based needs. If we understand the intent and needs behind the behavior and address those effectively, the behavior changes and the change will be without resistance and far more long lasting.

Using the late employee example, we would ask thoughtful questions to discover the intent, such as, "Can you share with me what is happening, either here at work or at home, that's contributing to your being late?" Say the employee reports that they have a sick child and it is taking extra time to get the child settled before leaving for work. This appears to be circumstantial so you explore further to determine the extent of the circumstance. What is the prognosis for the child? Is there anything you can do to help with the current situation? By understanding the circumstance and the extent of it, you can make adjustments that serve both the employee and the company.

Say, however, in seeking to understand the intent, the employee answers that he feels the work/life balance is off and that he is spending too much time on the job. This is not circumstantial, it's situational. Now you need to dig deeper and find out what needs and values drive this perception. Getting a different behavior might be as easy as helping this employee understand the value of the work he is doing or it might indicate a need to adjust his work schedule or situation so both he and the company are better served.

In any case, you will get a far better result if you are looking at and addressing intent, needs and values. You can never positively affect a behavior long-term by addressing the behavior itself. To get to the core where motivation occurs, you must get past behaviors and address the intent.

Avoiding Demotivators

Workplace dynamics have shifted dramatically recently because the newer generations aren't playing by the old rules and, try as they might, managers have been unable to change the behaviors of the younger generations. The result of trying is reflected in the *Gallup* polls and studies published by the *Society for Human Resource Management* (SHRM), which continue to show that the majority of employees are disengaged and disinterested in company goals and initiatives. SHRM reported that the turnover rate continues to increase and job satisfaction to decrease.

There are many factors driving job dissatisfaction, but one of the greatest is failure on the part of leaders and managers to understand and adjust to new and different values. Leaders, realizing the high cost of turnover and hoping to retain quality workers, keep scrambling to find ways to attract and retain them, but the methods they are using are not working, and probably never will.

The few organizations, such as Google, FaceBook, Zappos, Starbucks, Federal Express, and Costco, that have figured out how to motivate and manage the new workforce, are skyrocketing to success at unprecedented rates while those who still using the old established model seem helpless to stem the rising tide of losses.

The game-changer is the steady departure of one large cohort (Baby Boomers) and the rise of another (Millennials). Traditionalists, who shaped most of the organizations in the world today, are all but gone from the workplace. Baby Boomers, who now dominate management positions and have been a large percentage of the general workforce, are beginning to retire. Generation X and Millennials are entering the workplace in greater and greater numbers and will be the majority in the next ten to twelve years. That means organizations which were built around Traditional or Boomer values will soon no longer be relevant to the majority of the workforce, and this is a big problem since *relevance* is a big value for the largest generation in history; Millennials.

According to the U.S. Census Bureau, Millennials are 80 million strong compared to 78 million for Baby Boomers who previously held the largest generation record. Baby Boomers currently make up a large portion of the workforce and occupy most management positions so are still a dominant force in the workplace, but that won't be the case for long. Baby Boomers (born between 1946 and 1964) are now retiring at a rapid rate while Millennials (born between 1980 and 2000) are entering the workforce at an equally rapid rate. By 2025 the majority of Baby Boomers will be retired and the workplace will be filled with Millennials.

Though Generation X (born between 1965 and 1979) is a smaller cohort, they too hold very different values than those held by Baby Boomers and Traditionalists. Generation X gets less attention than Millennials for two reasons: they are a smaller cohort (only 28 million strong) and they are hard to define. They are generally described as a group of people who have pulled away from the idea of class, status, money and societal labels, hence the supposedly non-label name Generation X, and they prefer to remain non-descript. They relate more to Millennials than to Boomers and are more inclined to adopt Millennial values since they generally see Boomer values as too restrictive and hierarchical.

Failure to Understand Changing Values

Although Millennials are not yet the majority in the workplace, they are already the force that is reshaping it. Their values are driving massive business and political outcomes all over the world. The election and reelection of President Barack Obama, the "Arab Spring", and the protests and uprisings all over the globe are driven primarily by Millennials.

Neither Gen X nor Millennials tolerate business or political practices that fail to consider their needs, and they are not opposed to walking out the door of an organization or taking to the streets to make a point. And, when they walk out, they don't just walk out silently. They communicate their dissatisfaction through social media and can reach millions in mere minutes. The ability to broadcast their opinions and observations is one of the power shifters these generations fully understand and will continue to use. Organizations would be wise to consider how visible their actions are about to become and adjust accordingly.

There are still plenty of leaders and managers clinging to the hope that Gen Xers and Millennials will eventually "shape up." Don't be one of them. You can be certain it isn't going to happen in the way most hope or imagine. The direction toward which these generations are trending is quite clear if you are willing to see it. Realize that their core values are not going to change much as they mature. What has to change are business and leadership models. Be on the forefront of that change.

Overlooking the Diamonds

It is not uncommon for organizations to have plenty of the right workers already on board and not know it because they don't have a clear picture of the characteristics and attributes that work best in their particular environment. It is also not uncommon for companies to lose high potentials simply because they go unrecognized and remain highly underutilized.

Most organizations operate like the farmer in the tale once told by Russell Cromwell called *Acres of Diamonds*. In the story, a Persian farmer, named Al Haphid, sells his farm and goes in search of diamonds. He searches far and wide for years without success and finally, penniless and broken, leaps from a cliff to his death.

In the meantime, the man who bought Al Haphid's farm found a large diamond in the rough in the stream where he watered his livestock. He thought it attractive, but not knowing what it was, took it home and placed it on the fireplace mantle. There it sat for many years until a priest who recognized diamonds in the rough came visiting, saw the huge diamond on the mantle and, astonished to see such a find, asked the man where he got it.

It turned out that the land on which the farm was located was the great diamond mine of Galconda; the biggest diamond mine in the world. According to the story, the Koohinor diamond of England and the Orlov diamond of Russia, some of the most valuable crown jewels on earth came from the Galconda diamond mine.

Like Al Haphid, leaders are overlooking "diamonds in the rough" and continually searching for "diamonds" they recognize. It's an inefficient and expensive practice. Most organizations are filled with diamonds, but they never get a chance to shine.

Ineffective Leadership

Management woes are a constant source of discussion among people who post reviews on *Glassdoor.com*. Among the most frequent complaints are managers who micromanage, treat underlings like children or make extreme demands. Even C-level executives receive approval ratings as low as 19%. Ineffective leadership is the number one complaint and the number one reason given in exit interviews, for quitting a job. Whether this is fact or reality is irrelevant. What is relevant is that it is the prevailing perception and, as you are likely already aware, perception *is* reality; at least the reality that drives opinions, attitudes and behaviors.

Job Insecurity

Another source of frustration for the majority of the workforce is job insecurity. Workers say they don't trust management to support or protect them and many doubt management has the ability (or willingness) to keep the company competitive. So they doubt that their job or the company is secure.

Dish Network has had the unfortunate distinction of topping the list of companies despised by their workers for several years. According to a January 2013 article in Bloomberg Businessweek, Dish Network's management is inconsiderate to employees, customers, and shareholders alike. They called it "the meanest company in America" and cited employee complaints about the poor treatment, poor pay, and poor benefits they received in spite of the requirement of doing difficult work in unpleasant conditions. The reputation of Walmart is not too far behind.

The least satisfied workers are those whose jobs require them to interact with customers (sales representatives, customer service agents, and technicians). It doesn't take a lot of thought to realize that this is a very big problem. Underpaying any employee is unwise. It implies the employee is under-valued. Underpaying those who directly impact customer experiences is downright foolhardy. It doesn't matter how big the giant, when employees and customers begin abandoning an organization, its eventual demise is inevitable (The Meanest Company in America, 2013).

Income Disparity

Another source of widespread dissatisfaction, especially among younger workers including the last third of Baby Boomers, is income disparity. Jack Lowe, founder of TD Industries, a highly regarded company in Dallas, Texas says he has personally observed that motivation and engagement are directly affected by income disparity. Lowe found that, to the degree that the highest paid employee earned more than ten times the wages of the average employee, motivation and engagement declined. This aligns with research which reports that employees place the upper limit of income variance at a 10:1 ratio.

TD Industries has been on the *Fortune Best Places to Work* list every year since its inception. Clearly, Jack Lowe and the leaders he has trained are doing lots of things right. Income parity is one of them. None of the executives at TD Industries is paid more than ten times what an average worker is paid.

In the publicly traded organizations named on the *worst* places to work list, the CEO generally earns thousands of times more than the average worker and tens of thousands of times more than the lowest paid. Those leading these organizations keep looking for ways to get employees more engaged and productive, but it won't happen as long as such a large disparity exists, and high-paid CEOs have little interest in addressing this issue, much less correcting it. If any correction ever occurs, it will have to come from stockholder demands or the fact that these companies no longer exist.

This wasn't an issue in the past because the large disparity didn't exist. Today it's a big problem and getting bigger because Generation X and Millennials don't even bother to have a conversation about it. If they see a situation they consider unfair and unfixable, they simply walk off the job, often in groups, as happened at Journey's Mall in Rochester, New York in 2013 when employees crafted a big note to the insensitive manager, posted it on the door and the entire team walked out leaving the store unmanned and closed for business. Imagine the cost, not only in lost sales, but in poor public relations (it made national news) and in the cost to hire and train a new crew.

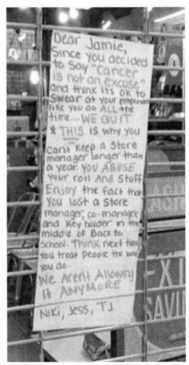

The newer generations broadcast their displeasure openly and actively. They realize that they have the ability to affect change on a large scale and they do a lot more than just post signs in protest. They spread the word on the internet, as the photo posted by *Huffington Post* shows. They take to the streets as they did during the Occupy Wall Street movement in 2012 and in other protest movements around the globe. They take pictures of events around them and post them immediately to YouTube, FaceBook, Pinterest, and other widely consulted mediums. And they aren't shy about speaking out against anyone, especially large organizations they believe act irresponsibly.

Article in The Huffington Post entitled *Journey's Mall Staff Quits in Most Epic Way Possible* by Catherine Taibi 09/03/2013

They can make things happen almost instantly, such as organizing "flash mobs" where groups of people, many of whom are strangers, show up and perform a predetermined activity. They can also alter awareness and buying habits with "cash mobs" where groups show up and buy from a predetermined place, usually a small, local merchant.

Big businesses and governments need to pay more attention to this. These are indicators of what is to come. The newer generations know how to redirect the flow of power and they are actively looking for ways to take full advantage of it.

Before the age of global communication people knew only what their leaders allowed them to know. Today, not even the most dictatorial of countries can keep their citizens from knowledge or from asserting their view.

Leaders, get ready. A power shift is upon you. Whether you are the head of a country, a company, a team or a family, you are at the precipice of a world-changing shift and it is far greater than most imagine.

CHAPTER SIX
The Performance Platform

While leaders cannot change the core values of their employees, they *can* influence employee performance and dedication through effective motivation methods and by making sure each employee is aligned in three vitally important areas. We consider these performance factors vital because to the degree any one of them is missing, the individual is ineffective. These three factors support the platform or foundation upon which all motivation and performance rests. With all three developed, even employees that were previously disengaged and struggling to keep up can become high performers.

The Three Vital Factors Are:

- Capacity
- Interest
- Skills

Capacity

Capacity is an innate factor that cannot be affected by external input. We are born with the capacity to do many things, but where we lack capacity, we cannot perform effectively in those particular areas even if the interest happens to be there. For example, if an individual lacks the temperament (natural capacity) for technology, typically, they lack interest in that area as well. Interest may be artificially induced through a belief that one *should* know about technology, but the individual will struggle to learn the skills and will apply them only as necessary. On the other hand, an individual with a natural capacity for technology will find learning it easy, which will increase both interest and effectiveness.

An example of interest where capacity is lacking is Alan who decided he wanted to be an outside salesperson because he believed he could make more money and have more flexibility in sales. He tried several sales jobs in several companies, but always underperformed because his natural temperament was conflict averse and any time a prospect challenged him, he would back down. He especially avoided answering objections and asking for the sale. As much as he wanted to be successful in sales, Alan was not able to get past the stress that came up around conflict or the anticipation of it, so he continued to struggle.

Interest and Skills

When employees are underperforming, usually the first thing managers do is provide them with some form of additional training. We have found this to be a backward and frequently counter-productive approach. Until employees are interested in learning, no real learning occurs. Until they are interested in doing a good job, all the training, coaching and pep talks are a waste of company resources.

Performance improvement plans are the approach of choice these days. Usually, they are structured communication tools designed to facilitate constructive discussion between the employee and the supervisor. They rarely produce the intended results. The primary reason is that performance improvement plans tend to focus on the wrong things. Generally, the focus is on skills performance and attitude and even if the feedback is not the typical "you need to improve your performance here and here" or "your attitude needs to improve," the communication is all but worthless if the employee is not interested.

The employee's *capacity* to do better is rarely addressed or even considered except in negative inquiries, such as "why do you continue to do this wrong?" What's generally missing from performance improvement plans is the driver of performance; *interest* in doing a great job. According to research by McKinsey & Company, in spite of more than two decades of intense performance improvement efforts, corporate reorganizations, new software systems, and quality-improvement projects, the failure rate of change initiatives remains around 70% on average (Keller and Aiken, 2000).

When interests are not addressed, even star performers begin to burn out and lose their edge. The performance matrix (*illustration 6.1*) shows the impact of interest and skills on performance. To have an organization filled with high performance people and high potentials on their way to stardom, the primary focus of organizations needs to be on priming interest, not on polishing skills.

The Performance Matrix

Skills Plus Interest

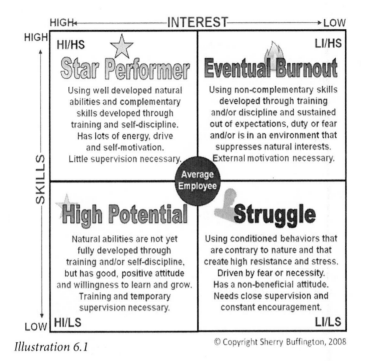

Illustration 6.1   © Copyright Sherry Buffington, 2008

The Performance Matrix shows the effect of two of the most essential factors for high performance; interest and skills. Notice that this matrix does not say "interests", but rather "interest." Interests can cover a lot of things. They can be mild interests or strong ones, work related or not. Most people have many interests; movies, music, sports, reading, nature, animals, people, and a whole array of other things. They are not necessarily motivated enough by each of the things they find interesting to keep at them long enough to become proficient, however.

"Interest," on the other hand, implies a deeper, more singular involvement. We maintain the kind of interest implied in the singular only insofar as the interest continues to meet our dominant needs and bring us satisfaction. This can be seen in everything from relationships, to play, to the work we do. We tend to maintain associations with people who continue to meet our needs and add to our sense of satisfaction, for instance, and to avoid or end relationships with people who don't. We also work and play at things that continue to meet our needs and add to our sense of satisfaction.

If interest is lacking, even things considered recreational are not pursued. Almost everyone can name leisure activities they have tried and decided were not enjoyable enough to continue doing. If loss of interest causes us to disengage from play, imagine what happens when we lose interest in the work we are doing or the environment in which we do the work. This happens in organizations all the time and, when it does, employers need to discover why interest has diminished and look for ways to reengage disinterested employees rather than subjecting them to more training.

Star Performers

Take a look at the matrix in *illustration 6.1*. Notice that the Star Performer in the upper left-hand section has the ideal combination of high interest and high skills combined with an innate capacity to apply both. This ideal combination only occurs when the developed skills are complementary to naturally preferred abilities (capacity) and where current conditions support interest. When job-related tasks complement both nature and training, and when leadership and the environment are also a good fit, fully engaged, high performing employees are the norm.

The Proficiency Trap and Burnout

Burnout occurs when skilled employees lose interest. Any adult of normal intelligence can learn skills over a relatively wide range and, once the skills are learned sufficiently well, the individual will test as having strength around that learned process. But strengths and motivators are two very different things.

For example, I (Sherry) have formal training in accounting and I'm good at crunching numbers, but I have little interest in it so I am not motivated to perform that job. When necessary, I can do the work and do it well for awhile, but it doesn't take long for me to move to Burnout (high skills/low interest) and lose momentum. Put me in front of a group where I am teaching and seeing people get real results and I have energy to spare at the end of the day.

Marc has really good presentation skills, but when he moves from right-brained, people-centric delivery into more structured and isolated left-brain development processes for long periods of time, his interest is challenged.

Both of us love training and development and creating products that quickly move people to high levels of effectiveness. We never lose the excitement of seeing leaders step into their real power or teams take quantum leaps to higher performance. These activities are naturally interesting. They feed our passion and align with our natural capacity to influence positive change.

Like us, many people are proficient at things for which they have no passion. We call this a *proficiency trap*, and people get caught in it all the time.

Two Reasons People Get Caught in Proficiency Traps

1. People tend to get reinforced for what they do well. Since we are all motivated to move away from pain and toward pleasure and the unconscious mind interprets reinforcement as pleasure, the praise we receive induces us to continue the behavior even when the activity is not personally pleasurable. Psychological pleasure (compliments and acceptance) can be just as intoxicating as physical or mental pleasure, but it is externally driven motivation and hard to sustain.

2. Learning goes from unconscious incompetence (we don't know that we don't know) to unconscious competence (we know how to do something well enough that we don't have to think about it anymore). Both unconscious incompetence and unconscious competence are comfortable states so we seek to maintain them. The two learning stages in between—conscious incompetence (we know that we don't know) and conscious competence (we still have to think our way through it)—are uncomfortable states, so we avoid those. On one end of the learning curve is ignorant bliss (unconscious incompetence) and on the other end is blissful proficiency. Learning a new skill takes us into the conscious place of discomfort and outside our comfort zone so we just keep doing what we already know how to do until the discomfort of doing it exceeds the discomfort of learning a new skill.

Motivation is sustained by natural interests, not by what an individual learns to do. Yet we get caught in proficiency traps because it's easier to keep doing what we know how to do, and easier to get hired for those already established skills.

Most employers don't even bother to look for what a job candidate is interested in. They only want to know what the candidate can do. Yet, when capabilities are not aligned with sustainable interest (natural abilities enhanced by complementary learned skills) at some point the individual will burn out. When they do, the typical response from an employer is to try to make the employee more capable and it rarely, if ever, works because what is needed is more interest.

Going back to the matrix, notice that Star Performers and High Potentials are on the left (high interest) side. Also notice that the employee at or approaching burnout has high skills, but low interest. It is not uncommon for employees to come into an organization as Star Performers and move to Burnout because the nature of the job, the environment, and/or leadership proves non-complementary. As organizational trainers,coaches and consultants, we have seen this occur so many times we have lost count.

There are three reasons why burnout occurs:

1. The job is not a good match—too many required tasks are unsatisfying or stress-producing
2. Leadership is ineffective
3. The environment is unhealthy

High Potentials

Another common mistake organizations make is assuming that their high potentials are people who are effective in some other position. While a good work ethic and past performance is a good predictor of future performance, it does not follow that the performance will carry over into another type of job or environment. It is not always possible to take high performers and cross train them into another position and have them excel in the new position. A common example of this is moving a star salesperson or the best technician into a management position where more often than not they soon begin to flounder. They were stars in the original position because that position brought all the right elements together. They flounder as managers because the management position requires skills which don't sustain interest and, in many instances, produce stress.

Strugglers

Organizations tend to look at employees that fit into the Struggler quadrant and assume the only thing they can or should do with these employees is get rid of them. That is not always the case. If the interest of such employees can be sparked, they can be moved from Struggler to High Potential. Then, all that is necessary is to provide them with the right training which, in their case, will have a powerful effect because the employee will be interested in learning. As interested employees gain the necessary skills, they begin moving up the scale toward Star Performer.

Except in the case of complex skills like medicine or engineering, it is always easier to teach skills to someone who has the interest than to try to interest someone with the skills but no natural inclination toward the task. In fact, it is not possible to create a Star Performer where there is insufficient interest unless the factors that prevent interest are eliminated.

Rarely is training alone a sufficient catalyst for awakening disengaged employees. Individual and group coaching tend to be much more effective because coaches have more time to assess individual and organizational dynamics and adjust their approach to fit needs. A good coach with the right tools can discover what truly interests the individual they are coaching and get them engaged before the learning process begins. Even here organizations are not likely to get the long term results they are hoping for unless the leaders are actively involved in creating a healthy culture and developing great leaders to sustain it.

Before any initiative will be effective, disengaged employees must be engaged or reengaged. To do that, leaders will need to take the time to discover what drives the kinds of employees they need, and find ways to provide it. Unfortunately, ordinary leaders have no interest in doing that. They argue that employees just need to follow the rules and do what is expected of them. It's a catch-22 because to effectively do what is expected of them, employees must be engaged and to be engaged they have to be interested.

Illustration 6.2 shows the four stages of learning and the effect of the three essential performance factors. In each graph, interest and commitment are high at the outset, but competence is low. In the first example, interest is not sustained through each stage so both commitment and competence drop. In the second example, interest is sustained and the learning curve looks very different. Where interest is sustained, commitment remains high and there is greater comittment to learning.

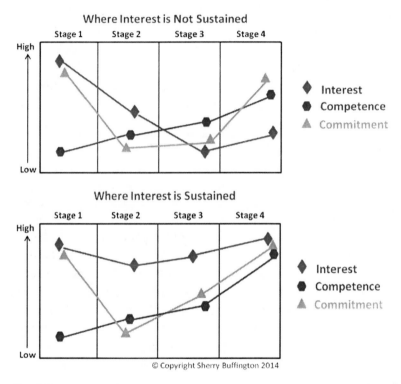

Illustration 6.2

Consider the common practice of moving someone who is proficient in technology into a people-focused management position. Technologically inclined people generally prefer managing processes so their interest in managing people is quite low. Even if commitment to the new job is initially high, it will wane in time and continuing to perform the job competently will be difficult.

This is a classic example of taking a high performer and advancing them to the level of incompetence and low performance. It is not uncommon to hear technically inclined people who have been promoted to management lament that they never wanted to be a manager. Generally, they would love to go back to the job where they felt competent, but don't know how to do that without losing face. We have seen many instances where a company lost a really good employee as a result of "promoting" the employee to a level of incompetence. This is what Peter Drucker referred to as the Peter Principle. It's an expensive blunder, not just in earnings, but in the loss of a once good employee. Morale, innovation, and employee engagement all plummet when there is a change in management too, which can adversely affect customer satisfaction and retention.

Competence and commitment without interest generally becomes a proficiency trap. People get stuck in proficiency traps when they learned a skill out of necessity or opportunity more than out of interest and are competent enough in that arena to function well enough to receive positive feedback for their skills. But, make no mistake; where interest is lacking, so too is high level competence. People stuck in a proficiency trap rarely perform to capacity.

Frustrated Leaders

Because organizations are focused on the wrong part of the formula (skills rather than interest), managers are often at a complete loss as to how to improve performance. They keep prodding and training and adding what they believe are incentives, but their employees remain disengaged. Many managers report with great frustration that their efforts have been about as effective as butting their heads against a brick wall. Here's why: like the technologist turned manager, most employees really do want to do a good job. They almost always come in the door with great hopes and expectations, and it usually takes a lot to cause them to shut down.

The main reason disinterest occurs is that the requirements of the job don't fit the natural inclinations of the individual. Other reasons are being pushed to perform without being given the resources needed to do a good job and being made to feel like a commodity whose only value is to serve the company's interests. Even where there is job fit, employees report that they resent being treated as nothing more than a "human resource" for company profit.

We once went into an organization as consultants/coaches to the heads of several departments. In every department we heard horror stories about how the company's disconnected and completely out of touch CEO was wreaking havoc and preventing progress. The team leaders in the product development division reported that they were extremely frustrated because just the week before we arrived they had met with the CEO and he had finally conceded that the project they had been working on for more than two years needed to be scrapped. The engineers had known almost from day one that the project would not fly and they had collectively and individually informed the CEO of that fact in an effort to redirect it toward a more successful outcome. They had presented a workable plan that would have resulted in a functional product, shortened delivery time and saved the company a lot of money, but the executive quickly discounted their expertise, ignored their advice and insisted that they pursue things his way.

By the time the project got scrapped they had wasted more than two years and untold resources. Worse, in spite of all they had done to prevent the losses, when the CEO finally decided the project had to be scrapped, he accused the engineers of sabotaging it to prove that they were right. When they protested and presented evidence to the contrary, the CEO recanted but stated he believed the project failed because the team had not tried hard enough.

Were these engineers disengaged? Not completely, but without intervention they soon would have been. They were still feeling and expressing anger, disappointment and frustration over the time and resources that had been wasted, and these are not emotions that come from completely disengaged employees. Completely disengaged employees don't even bother to express their anger anymore because they don't feel any. Any passion they might have had for making a contribution to the company is gone and they no longer care whether the company is wasting time and resources. All disengaged employees want to do is put in their time, collect their paycheck and sleepwalk through the day until it's time to go home.

While rules, procedures and clear guidelines are necessary and desirable to maintain structure and order, they need to serve the people as well as the organization. If they don't, they destroy initiative and kill any interest employees may have had in the job, the company, and the company's goals. Once disengagement sets in, any possibility of having an organization filled with high performing employees becomes little more than fanciful imagination. Interest is a critically important factor for performance. Without it, all the skills training in the world won't produce a star performer.

Because the causes of employee problems can be broad and varied, and each of the three performance factors impacts the others, the exact cause may at first be hard to pinpoint. Though the source of employee ineffectiveness is always either lack of interest or lack of skills, when the cause is lack of interest, as it usually is, it is often necessary to dig deeper to discover the reasons.

Disinterest has three basic causes: the environment, leadership (either the direct manager or top management) and poor job fit. Poor performance can certainly occur because the employee is generally difficult, but whatever the cause, it must always be cured at the source and leaders are the ones who must make those calls. They either tolerate the behavior or take steps to correct it. New systems, re-engineering, quality circles, team-building exercises, incentives, raises, and all the other things that are commonly tried are temporary fixes at best. For sustainable results, the source of the problem must be addressed and corrected.

Generally, leaders are well aware of the cost in time and money of a failed project and they generally know the cost of employee turnover. What they often don't know is why their efforts are not working the way they want or what to do about it. So let's explore that.

Conscious Intent Versus Subconscious Function

What we generally refer to as genius is the perfect alignment of natural capacity, high interest and good skills training. Like a three-legged stool, you cannot stay seated comfortably for long if all three legs are not there. Before long the effort required to keep the stool upright becomes too much and you lose your balance, not because you want to, but because you are out of energy and, once energy drops, performance drops with it.

No performance improvement program will improve performance where *interest* or natural *capacity* for a particular skill set is missing.

Without these, no amount of training will produce high quality, sustainable results. No matter what the individual's conscious intent or how much coaching and training is provided, once energy is depleted in a particular endeavor, the subconscious mind, which is intent on conserving energy, redirects the individual into another, more energy sustaining state and interest in continuing to learn in that particular area diminishes.

Let's say, for example, that the purpose of a performance improvement program is to improve the performance of a quality control inspector, but the inspector is distractible and does not have the natural capacity to attend to detail closely. While in training and while being carefully supervised, he might be vigilant and performance will improve. Over time, however, the effort required to continue attending to detail will become too great and he will again become distracted and even more disinterested in performing the job because his perception of what he *should* be able to do, but can't, increases his stress levels, which further decreases focus. The result is a downward spiral where performance continues to drop off until he either quits or gets fired.

Subconscious processes prevent most people from effectively repeating what they perceive as a failed effort. So, if the initial training fails, attempting to reinforce the earlier behaviors using the same methods will bring up resistance few can get past because once a failed attempt brings up resistance, future attempts along the same lines take even more time and effort.

Studies suggest that about 30% of employees improve as a result of typical performance improvement initiatives. Those who do have the natural capacity and the interest they need (legs 1 and 2) to succeed. All they are missing is the skills training. But skills training should always be the *third* consideration. The first consideration needs to be whether those being targeted for performance improvement have the natural capacity and secondly whether they have the interest. Influencing high performance is not possible where capacity and interest are lacking.

When employee performance drops, or never gets up to speed, the reason is rarely lack of technical know-how. Unless organizations are just hiring warm bodies and not doing due diligence in the hiring process, poor performance is almost always due to lack of capacity or lack of interest, and skills training won't correct that.

Consider the case of a previously high performing salesman whose sales had dropped off dramatically. The salesman hadn't offered any explanation for the drop other than that he was trying to get readjusted to a recent change in territory. When sales didn't improve over several months, the sales manager devised a performance improvement plan which focused on adjusting the salesman's attitude and reassessing his skills. After four months of interventions and little difference in the sales numbers, we were called in to help. Within an hour we had the answer. The real cause of the drop in sales was loss of interest. This had contributed to the shift in attitude the sales manager had observed, but that was a *result*, not the cause, and effective change cannot be made by addressing the result. The salesman was still very interested in serving his customers and he still strongly believed in the products he was selling. His loss of interest was so deep and subtle that even he was unaware of it until he looked at it.

Interest had dropped off when the sales manager had arbitrarily decided to cut the salesman's territory and, in the division, had given some of his favorite customers to a new and relatively green salesperson. The cut in territory felt like a penalty for high performance and the loss of customers he cared about and had nurtured for years with no consideration for him or the relationship he had with his customers had taken the wind out of his sails.

The sales manager was after greater saturation and had assumed incorrectly that a smaller territory would allow this top performer to increase market share. Until the cause of his loss of interest was adequately addressed and adjustments made, nothing the sales manager could have done would have improved the salesman's performance. Fortunately, this sales manager was wise enough to acknowledge his mistake and make corrections. Within days the salesman was back on track and, at the end of the following quarter had exceeded himself. The reason, he reported, was because knowing the sales manager had his best interests at heart and was willing to do the right thing had made him all the more delighted to be working for that company. Bottom line: knowing the sales manager had his back had increased his level of interest and with the increased interest came increased performance.

In the example of the QC inspector, *capacity* was lacking. In the case of the salesperson, capacity was there, but *interest* was lacking. Knowing the cause of a drop in interest is the first step in rekindling it. Appreciative inquiry is a good way to discover the cause as long as it is focused on interest. Most performance improvement plans tend to focus on skills or attitude. Those administereing them tend to assume that capacity has already been demonstrated and interest a given if the employee is still on the job. Such assumptions can foster resentment and lead to lowered performance rather than improvement.

In appreciative inquiry, the individual's capacity to perform will naturally surface so questions are not directed to capacity. Instead, the questions are specific to interest, intent and personal needs. Appreciative inquiry asks questions such as:

- Do you still like working for the company?
- Are you enjoying your job?
- Are there parts of your job that you find difficult or stressful?
- Is there something about the way *we* do business that doesn't work for you?
- Do you still believe our products and services provide real value to the customer?
- Do you feel supported here?
- What do you need that you are not currently getting?
- Has something changed that has affected the way you feel about your job?

Not only can appreciative inquiry help you get to the heart of the matter, it can also save you a lot of time and money on development costs. A "no" answer to the question "Are you still excited by the challenge of selling our products in the marketplace" from a salesperson for example, would make it clear that no amount of training would make a difference. The best approach here would be to shift your focus to discovering why the thrill is gone. You might discover that the employee is in the wrong job, which would allow both you and the employee to make adjustments that would better serve you both. Or you might discover that there is a flaw in your product or company that needs correcting.

ROI: Training That Gets Results

A study done in 2006 and reported on by *Chief Learning Officer Magazine* suggested that in most organizations, in-class training produces the desired result only about 20% of the time (Whitney 2006). That figure includes technical training as well as soft skills training.

A study on the effect of online training conducted by Croft-Baker for Motorola in 2001, found that online, self-paced training got even worse results than in-class training. That study showed that 60% of employees who registered for e-learning never even start their training and fewer than 25% of those who started, finished it, which factors to a completion rate of less than 10% of online learners. With imporved online learning, things have certainly improved since that study, but not enough.

According to the *American Society for Training and Development*, U.S. firms spent more than $156 billion on employee development in 2012 and the researchers assert that in any given year 90% of new skills training is lost within the year. Add this to the poor results of training indicated in the other studies and it becomes evident why organizations continue to invest billions of dollars in training and lament that they get very little return on their investment.

Employees want, need and expect training, especially the Millennial generation. Millennials say they are willing to stick with a job only as long as they are learning and growing. To keep these young people longer than a year or two, organizations are going to have to make sure they provide continual improvement. But, if typical training isn't the answer, what is?

After years of researching performance factors, Sherry developed the Performance Matrix to help explain why training and other performance improvement measures so frequently fail *(see illustration 6.1, chapter 6)*. In any performance improvement program, the first order of business has got to be creating conditions that keep employees interested and engaged. Disinterested employees don't bother to learn what they are directed to learn. They simply show up and bide their time. Before you invest in general training, discover the natural capacities of your people and align these with what they are interested in. Remember, the vital combination is capacity, interest and skills, in that order.

Most training decisions are made backwards. Managers look at poor performers and decide they need more training. But, what moves people from being merely trained to high performance is *practice*, and people won't practice if they are not first interested in applying what they have learned. Further, practice won't yield a great result if the one practicing lacks the capacity to perform well in that role or skill. No amount of training will produce a high performer if the trainee lacks the capacity to perform or the interest to put what they have learned into practice.

The High Performance Formula

People don't perform when they lack interest or when they don't believe they are competent to manage a task. Interest creates the desire to learn where the perception of competence provides the impetus to keep going; to keep trying and practicing and polishing to a level of expertise.

The High Performance Formula is:

- Perception of Capacity + Interest = Commitment to Learn
- Commitment + Training = Confidence
- Confidence + Desire to Excel Leads to Practice
- Practice Leads to Competence

The Ten Most Valued Competencies

	Competencies	Requirements (in order of importance)
1	The Ability to Communicate Clearly and Effectively	Personal Development, EQ, Communications/listening training
2	The Ability to Relate to Others Well Individually and in Teams	Personal Development, EQ. Training for some
3	Honesty, Integrity, Ethics	Personal Development, EQ
4	Good Judgment and Accountability	Personal Development, EQ
5	Ability to Make Independent Decisions and Problem-Solve	Personal Development, EQ, Training for some
6	Innovation and Risk-Taking	Personal Development, EQ, Training for some
7	Commitment and Dependability	Personal Development, EQ
8	Determination and Initiative	Personal Development, EQ
9	Ability and Willingness to Follow Protocol	Personal Development, EQ
10	Business/Job Acumen	Job Specific Training, Personal Development, EQ,

© Copyright Sherry Buffington 2009

Illustration 6.3

Competence

Over the years we have asked hundreds of leaders what they look for in employees. The competencies listed in *illustration 6.3* were compiled from the answers we received over a twenty year period.

Notice that only the *last item* on the list requires specific job skills training. Personal development levels and emotional intelligence (EQ) are the most important factors in nine of the ten competencies and these cannot be taught, but *they can be developed*. Providing additional training for an individual with low EQ and/or low personal development typically only builds resentment and fosters bad attitudes.

To ensure high levels of performance, personal development, emotional intelligence, natural traits and job skills training are all essential and all must be aligned to the job and the company's culture. When they are, any reasonably intelligent person can be successful.

Unfortunately, most of the methods organizations use to select, promote or develop employees don't provide sufficient insight into personal development and competency-specific emotional intelligence. To be sure you have the right employees in the right seats, it's important to get beneath the surface and gain an accurate measure of these essential factors. If you are interested in deeper insights into yourself and your people, take a few minutes to explore CORE assessments. You can learn more about them at www.starperformancesystems.com or scan the QR code.

Personal Development and Emotional Intelligence

Where personal development and emotional intelligence (EQ) come into the High Performance Formula is at the practice point. It takes discipline to apply oneself to any endeavor and self-discipline comes as we develop our positive personal traits and emotional intelligence.

Emotional intelligence is defined as the ability to effectively monitor one's own emotions and the emotions of others, and to use the information to guide one's thinking and actions. EQ is a fairly specific ability that connects a person's knowledge processes to his or her emotional processes. EQ is different from emotions, emotional styles, emotional traits, and the traditional measures of intelligence based on general mental or cognitive ability (IQ). EQ involves a set of skills or abilities that are generally categorized into five domains:

- **Self-awareness**: Observing self and recognizing feelings as they occur.

- **Managing emotions**: Appropriately expressing emotions; realizing the cause or source of a feeling; handling fears, anxieties, anger, frustration, sadness, and other non-beneficial emotions effectively.

- **Motivating oneself**: Channeling emotions in the service of a goal; emotional self-control; delaying gratification for the long-term good; controlling impulses.

- **Empathy**: Sensitivity to the feelings and concerns of others; understanding their perspective; appreciating the differences in how people feel about things.

- **Relationship Competence**: Managing interactions with others; social capacity/skills.

Personal development and emotional intelligence levels are directly correlated with performance and overall effectiveness. Unfortunately, most of the measures used in organizations today don't allow leaders to look deeply enough to determine how well or poorly these two critical

factors are developed. Fortunately, the CORE assessments provide that feedback in specifically measurable and trackable ways.

Recap

To get employees to do what you want them to do, the first place to look is at their competence to perform the task, and then at their interest in doing it. You cannot get people to act by focusing on the action itself. Action is the *effect*. Competence (natural capacity plus learned skills) combined with interest is the *cause*.

To survive and thrive in the emerging marketplace, companies need innovative and creative people at both the employee and leadership levels. Selecting and leading people the old way won't work nor will it provide the results the marketplace demands.

Core values and the global meme, or mindset, are shifting and along with them so too is power. More than ever, the power lies in the minds of the people. In an information-based world, it is minds not hands that need to be understood and managed, and they are best managed from a well-balanced platform, which can only be maintained by a self-regulated, emotionally intelligent leader.

Self-regulated, emotionally intelligent leaders inspire trust and their predictable behaviors have a positive ripple effect across the company, just as the behaviors of a hot-head has a negative effect. Emotionally intelligent leaders are able to sustain safe, fair, structured freedom environments where drama and politics are very low and productivity very high. Top performers flock to these organizations and are not likely to leave them.

"We've reached the end of incrementalism. Only those companies that are capable of creating industry revolutions will prosper in the new economy."

Gary Hamel

"Smart people instinctively understand the dangers of entrusting our future to self-serving leaders who use our institutions, whether in the corporate or social sectors, to advance their own interests."

James C. Collins

CHAPTER SEVEN
Enforced Versus Legitimate Power

Over the years we have found three basic types of leaders. We call them Enforcers, Abdicators and Influencers. Only one of them is truly effective.

Enforcers are Theory X managers who believe that people are basically lazy and need to be pushed to perform. They believe they must force people to do what needs to be done and that's what they do. This produces fear and resistance rather than motivation to perform, however, so this type of manager generally gets 40% or less of their employees' performance capacity. The environment created by this type of manager is either a No Mistakes or a Firefighter culture.

In a No Mistakes culture people get called out for any mistake they make so they don't dare innovate or take risks. Everything is by the book, even if the book is outdated and ineffective. In a Firefighter culture no one has time to innovate. They are all too busy running around putting out fires. Enforcers create environments that have too many rules with overly strict boundaries and too little freedom.

Abdicators are weak or laissez-faire leaders who generally let their employees decide their own actions, but don't provide them with clear, firm boundaries to work within. They either believe that people work best when left to their own devices or they lack the courage to make hard decisions and hold people accountable. The reality is that effective teams need both flexibility and structure. Without clear and consistent application of rewards and consequences, and without solid boundaries to work within, employees feel uncertain and unmotivated to perform. This produces a No Consequence culture where even slackers have little to no consequences and where high performers soon lose heart. Why make the effort to perform well when slackers get the same benefits as performers? Abdicators create environments where there is too much freedom and too few rules and boundaries.

Though these two styles mismanage in polar opposite ways, both create fear which leads to high stress, low productivity, resentment and disengagement. Polls conducted by the *Gallup* Organization have reflected a largely disengaged workforce since the year 2000 with the disengagement rate hovering around 70% with every poll. The 2014 the poll showed:

Employees in General

- Engaged employees – 31 %
- Not-engaged employees – 51%
- Actively Disengaged – 17%

Government Employees

- Engaged employees – 27 %
- Not-engaged employees – 53%
- Actively Disengaged – 19%

Not-engaged means the employee is under-performing. Actively disengaged means the employee is purposely sabotaging the company, their boss, their team and/or their job. What's scary is that in these polls more than 70% of the workforce actually admits to under-performing or actively undermining the company. The numbers could be worse.

Gallup reports "While the state of the U.S. economy has changed substantially since 2000, the state of the American workplace has not. Currently, only 30% of the U.S. workforce is engaged in their work. The vast majority of U.S. workers (70%) are not reaching their full potential — a problem that has significant implications for the economy and the individual performance of American companies."(*Gallup*, Inc. *State of the American Workplace, 2013*)

Year after year this figure holds true. It is estimated that disengaged employees are costing organizations approximately $350 billion per year and taxpayers about $18 billon per year.

To re-engage employees, Enforcers and Abdicators are going to have to learn some new skills. But before they can do that, most are going to have to remove their blinders and adjust their attitude. In our experience, that's a tall order for most. It requires a level of emotional maturity and self-awareness that most people protecting big egos don't posess.

Influencers get to know their people. They choose their employees wisely and trust them to do a good job, and they give them plenty of freedom to produce within clearly defined parameters. Influencers know that to get the best from their people, they need to understand them. They implement procedures that let them know the natural skills, strengths, interests and capacity of each of their people. Their style is collaborative rather than dictatorial (No Mistakes/Firefighter) or laissez faire (No Consequences). They are effective at connecting people to one another and to their own best selves in ways that produce high levels of enthusiasm, engagement, commitment and performance.

As Generation X and Millennials take over the work force, this is the only style that will get results. Influencers create a healthy culture we call Structured Freedom where freedom and flexibility are balanced with well-defined boundaries and rules that are beneficial to everyone. High performers and high potentials thrive in this kind of culture.

In a Structured Freedom environment boundaries are clear, and rewards and consequences are clearly spelled out and consistently adhered to so everyone knows exactly what to expect. Yet, within these clear boundaries, there is a lot freedom and flexibility in the way one gets his or her job done.

Influencers have taken the best of the theory X and Y styles and combined them into a healthy whole. In an Influencer culture employees have the strong leadership espoused by theory X advocates and the trust and freedom espoused by theory Y advocates. This healthy combination, which we call Theory Z, pays big dividends.

The employees of Influencers are fiercely loyal to their leader and to the company they call home, and the strong revenue and profit figures that companies led by Influencers report make it clear the employees are committed to ensuring that the company succeeds.

Illustration 7.1 provides a more in-depth view of each style. Overall the Enforcer uses a negative approach, the Abdicator takes a neutral approach and the influencer takes a positive approach. Currently, the Enforcer style is by far the most used even though it is not producing engaged employees who perform at optimal levels.

Leader Style	Enforcer (Negative)	Abdicator (Neutral)	Influencer (Positive)
Induces Action Through	Guilt, Fear, Force	Guilt, Weak Influence	Strong Influence
Primary Method	Coercion	Manipulation	Inspiration
Environment Created	No Mistakes Firefighter	No Consequences Firefighter	Healthy Productive
Motivation	Low – Extrinsic Hard to Sustain	Low – Extrinsic Hard to Sustain	High – Intrinsic Easy to Sustain
Focus	Control, Tactics, procedures	Ease, Conflict Avoidance	Potential Possibilities
Approach	Aggressive Passive/Aggressive	Passive Passive/Aggressive	Assertive
Under Stress	Becomes More Aggressive	Becomes More Passive	Remains Assertive
Communication Style	Tell, No Discussion	Tell/Ask Low Feedback	Appreciative Inquiry
Style Produces	Resistance, High Turnover	Frustration, High Turnover	Self-motivation, Performance
Intention	Resistance, High Turnover	Frustration, High Turnover	Self-motivation, Performance
Supports Innovation	No	No	Yes
Knows Their People	No – Think they don't need to	No – Don't bother	Yes – to stay aligned/relevant
Effect	Burn Out - Struggle	Burn Out - Struggle	Star Performers High Potentials
Result	Compliance low Fear high	Compliance low Frustration high	Compliance high Motivation high
Competencies Supported	Job-related skills	none	All
Commitment and Trust	Next to none	Low	High
% of Leaders	63%	30%	7%

© Copyright Sherry Buffington and Marc Schwartz 2013

Illustration 7.1

The VIP Leader

Having spent ten years studying leaders and the factors that lead to greatness, we found that the most effective leaders are progressive visionaries who see leadership as an opportunity to positively influence people and help them be their best, rather than as a platform from which they can exert power. Being progressive, they see way beyond systems and the next quarter's numbers. They see the bigger picture and the longer view and their people are always right at the center of the vision. Because our research found that the primary factors for these highly effective leaders are vision, influence, and progressiveness, we call them VIP leaders.

One big, bold example of a company led by a progressive leader is Crete Carriers out of Nebraska. While driving down I-35 at different times, from different places and on totally unrelated trips, we each noticed and were intrigued enough by the message we saw on the back and sides of Crete Carrier trucks to independently make note of it. Marc even took pictures. Apparently so did many others as we found the following pictures online.

Although to most companies, this might seem like a terrible waste of advertising real estate, imagine the attitude of the guy driving the truck. Imagine the thoughts that go through the minds of truck drivers who work for less progressive companies when they see this message.

Imagine the numbers of people just like us who see that bold expression of employee appreciation and think, "I *like* that company." Imagine the feel for this company in the community where they are headquartered. Imagine the business that might come their way from progressive companies who ship products.

Because we are always trying to understand what makes companies tick (or fail to), we took the next step and researched Crete Carriers. Their people-centric approach was immediatley apparent in their philosophy.

Crete's Principles

We like to say, "There are no shortcuts" on our road to success and we practice that commitment by following these seven principles:

- We stress safety first and foremost. We never compromise the safety of our people or those with whom we share the road.

- We say what we mean and mean what we say. We deliver on the promises we make.

- We are ethical - we always do what is right. Even when no one is watching, our ethics demand that we always do the right thing.

- We follow the road less traveled. We stress long-term performance over short-term gains.

- We strive to be the best trucking company in the country. Not the biggest, but the very best in everything we do.

- We exercise mutual respect. We earn it through our actions and show it through our deeds.

- We have FUN! We work and play hard, but we remember to enjoy what we do.

This is a philosophy almost anyone can get enthused by. The big question is, if you were looking for a company to work for or do business with, would a company with this philosophy and approach interest you?

Another example is Vineet Nayar, CEO of an India-based global information company called HCL Technologies. In an interview with Nayar *Forbes Magazine* (June 2010) asked him about his employees first, customers second leadership philosophy. He answered, "We have found that the employees first approach produces far more passion than any motivational or recognition program. Why? Because it proves that management understands the importance of the work being done by the employees in the value zone. It demonstrates that we are actively helping them in ways that make it easier for them to do their jobs. It shows that we trust them to do what needs to be done in the way they believe it should be done. And it shows that we respect them for the value they bring to the company."

Companies such as Crete Carriers and HCL Technologies model the Structured Freedom business strategies which need to become the rule rather than the exception as Millennials and the generations who follow them dominate the workplace. This model will not be an option in the future because this is the leadership style Millennials insist upon, and thier tendency to walk out the door where they don't find it will prove very costly and, in many cases deadly, to companies who fail to adopt the Influencer leadership style.

Influencers have legitimate power. Enforcers and Abdicators have enforced power, and enforced power produces results only when the pressure is on.

Interestingly, Enforcers and Abdicators don't seem to have a model for the kind of healthy environment Influencers create. Both Enforcers and Abdicators think "structure" means rigid organizational rules with strict 9 to 5 work hours spent under the watchful eye of a supervisor in siloed departments. They have no idea how structure and freedom can coexist.

Influencers understand that flexibility and structure actually go hand in hand, as long as it is the right kind of structure. True structure has nothing to do with 9-5 work hours, complex organizational layers or close supervision. It is actually crystal clear expectations built around reasonable deadlines, and specific, measurable goals that everyone understands.

Influential leaders provide clarity and consistency, and balance it with support and guidance. Within that structure, employees are free to figure out how to execute actions that will advance the company's goals and achieve the best possible outcome.

Ultimately, influence is the only legitimate power there is, especially in a world that revolves around thought and innovation. In this world, organizations rise or fall depending on how effectively they engage the minds and hearts of their people. And engaging hearts is a lot more important than managers in most organizations assume because emotions increase or reduce stress. A stressed brain is a non-thinking, reactionary brain, and that generally leads to problems, not progress.

"The key to successful leadership today is influence, not authority."

Ken Blanchard

"People are never able to outperform their self-image."

John C. Maxwell

CHAPTER EIGHT
The Litmus Test

In chapter two, we explored Genghis Khan's now obsolete leadership model. Now let's examine a model that worked in the past and is still working today, the Disney model. This model was designed to maximize innovation. In Disney's time, the industrial model was still the norm and his model was a quite unique one. Disney wanted innovative, creative types who could think way outside the box and, being such a person himself, he knew the kind of management most organizations were using would not work for the kind of people he wanted to attract and retain.

Disney built his vision around four pillars which he clearly defined and regularly conveyed to his entire staff. The pillars were Dream, Believe, Dare and Do. Each of these terms encourages innovation and high performance thinking, which is exactly what Disney had in mind.

In Disney's time, most companies ignored the Disney model assuming it worked only in the entertainment industry. Today, engaging the minds and imagination of employees is essential and the Disney approach is a good one for any company seeking to attract and keep today's top talent. The Disney model has been adopted with great success by other progressive companies that realize its value in today's information age.

Though it might be possible to force people to run a production line faster, it is not possible to force cutting-edge thinking, innovation or creativity. The only way to get that is to engage minds. Disney was a master at that as is evidenced by the masterful model he built, which still supports innovation and inspires greatness.

One thing Disney did consistently was share his vision, his dreams, his goals and his values with his employees. Had he not done that, the four pillars, no matter how lofty sounding, could not have inspired the masterpieces Disney and his team turned out.

When companies fail to convey their values, vision, mission and dream to job candidates or employees, they often end up with employees whose values, interests, vision and goals don't align with those of the company. There are countless examples of people who were high performers in one culture and who fell far short of expectations in another because the organization either didn't know its mission and purpose, or it failed to convey them.

A recent example of this is Ron Johnson, the former CEO of JC Penney who was brought over from Apple. Under his leadership the company made some huge and very costly mistakes. They spent a lot of money foolishly trying to change their image and attract a younger client base and, in the process, lost most of their loyal customers and billions of dollars.

It doesn't take a lot of thought to realize that Johnson was out of his element. Apple, being an electronics giant that designs products which appeal to the technically savvy younger generations, fit Johnson's vision perfectly. Clothing, especially the lines of clothing JC Penney carried for years and had built their customer base around, was a whole different story. Because the company was not clear on who they were, what they stood for and who they served, they were able to be swayed way off-course by Johnson's misaligned vision.

JC Penney founder, James Cash Penney, had a service philosophy and clear ideas about what that meant. Some of his quotes reveal his basic philosophies and they are good ones, but they don't provide a compass to keep the company on course. For example:

"A merchant who approaches business with the idea of serving the public well has nothing to fear from the competition."

"Give me a stock clerk with a goal and I'll give you a man who will make history. Give me a man with no goals and I'll give you a stock clerk."

"Do not primarily train men to work. Train them to serve willingly and intelligently."

"In retailing, the formula happens to be a basic liking for human beings, plus integrity, plus industry, plus the ability to see the other fellow's point of view." (Penney quotes, 2011)

Though James Penney conveyed how to serve, he didn't clearly convey *who* the company was serving so switching gears to serve a new generation was actually not in conflict with the basic philosophy. Johnson apparently saw an emerging generation and decided serving it was a good idea, but the result was devastating. Had there been clarity around the fact that the company served the mainstream market with mid-priced products and that their target market was heads of family households, perhaps Johnson would not have been allowed to head in the direction he did.

The point to remember here is to be sure you clearly convey not just the company's vision, but also *who* you want to serve and *why*. When companies don't know why they exist, and for whom, or don't convey that to their people, all kinds of things can go wrong, not the least of which is an ever widening gap between management and staff.

In my book, *Exiting OZ*, I (Sherry) tell of an experience I had with one company which became the catalyst for carefully choosing the organizations we work with. This company, a public utility, was having huge problems with its employees. The problems had existed for some time and, in an effort to improve employee attitudes and behaviors without senior management having to make any changes, the organization had spent nearly eight million dollars to install a program they called "The Power of One." Everyone in the organization had to go through this program—except for senior management—though they understood the program and used the language of "One" in their many unproductive rah-rah meetings which they mistakenly believed would "fire up the troops." The result of the eight million dollar program was that three years later the employees were *less* productive and more uncooperative than ever.

It was at the point of near mutiny that I was recommended to the company's CEO by a client. I met with him and his senior management team to discuss the issues and possible solutions and they shared the story of how they had invested all this money in their employees and how the employees were now even worse and that they were at a loss as to what to do next.

With the CEO's permission, I conducted confidential interviews with some of the department heads and with first line employees to get a feel for what was going on. They all told essentially the same story. There was a huge gap between senior management and the rest of the employees, which the middle managers and several of the more outspoken employees had tried to get corrected for years.

Management continued to ignore the big gap and employee suggestions for bridging it. Instead, they decided to implement the eight million dollar program without consulting any of the managers or employees. The employees saw that as just the latest "slap in the face."

Requiring the participation of all employees and excluding upper management led the employees to see the program as nothing more than another manipulation. To make matters worse, after the program had been implemented, whenever the employees complained to senior management about the gap that continued to be the problem, they were reminded of all the money the company had "invested" in them and told that they should be grateful. But they weren't grateful, they were *furious* that management was now using the "joke of a program" to try to manipulate them. They were insulted that management thought they were gullible enough to buy into "the power of one" façade where no real or substantial change had actually taken place. "Oh, there's a 'power of one' alright," one department head told me. "It's the guy at the top pulling all the strings and, believe me, as long as he's there, nothing will change."

When I reported back to the CEO what I had discovered and suggested that the gap had to be bridged to solve the problem, the CEO was not happy with the report to say the least. Before I could even present my recommendations, he rose from his chair and slammed his fist on the conference table so hard that I and several of the senior managers in the room jumped. "I have been running this company for 22 years and doing a damn good job of it," he raged, "and I am not about to change what works! Can you fix those people or not?"

Clearly what he had been doing was *not* working or he wouldn't have been facing a near mutiny. My reply to "can you fix those people?" was, "No sir, I can't, because they aren't broken. What's broken is the means of communicating and connecting in meaningful ways and, to fix that, we need to start at the top; with you and other senior leaders."

The CEO was unwilling to entertain the idea of making any changes at the top. He was doing fine, he contended. He was not the problem. Without top down cooperation and participation, I knew our team would be wasting the organization's time and money and that would have been out of integrity for me, so I declined to take on the assignment.

Not surprisingly, the best employees continued to jump ship at the first opportunity and the remaining ones continued to work at 20% of their real capacity. Less than three years after that meeting, the company was out of business and another utility had taken over the area they once served.

This was a pivotal experience for me and one not unfamiliar to Marc. We had both worked with dysfunctional organizations led by non-progressive leaders where helping employees become more committed to high performance, increasing their awareness of their capabilities and worth, and helping them gain greater self-confidence typically resulted in the best and brightest leaving the organization to work for healthier companies where they were valued and appreciated.

Our goal has always been to help the our clients attract and *retain* the best talent, but in organizations where leaders were disconnected and unwilling to participate the best and brightest weren't staying once they gained greater confidence, which created a real dilemma for us. Although the move was best for the employee, it was not for the company, and the company was our client. This only occurred in companies where leaders were non-participative. In progressive, people-centric organizations, this never happened. Where leaders were willing to improve their leadership skills and participate in creating a healthier environment, the employees were happy to stay. The increased capabilities we helped employees develop not only made them more productive, it also made them happier and more determined to help their leader succeed.

Seeing the difference, we decided to stop working with organizations led by dysfunctional, disconnected leaders who are unwilling to change. I developed the *Organizational pH Litmus Test* to evaluate the companies we take on as clients and we began selecting our clients based on whether their leaders pass the litmus test.

Today we only work with companies whose leaders are committed to moving their organization into the Gold Zone and are willing to participate in the process. We have found that, no matter where a company is on the Litmus Scale at the outset, when leaders are committed to getting the organization into the Gold Zone—that healthy space where organizations can and do thrive, performance skyrockets.

The Organizational pH scale does more than just define the ideal range, it helps organizations determine where they fall within that range and in which direction to head to get to the gold. Take a look at the scale and see how your organization measures up.

The Gold Zone on the Organizational pH Scale is what Greek Philosopher, Aristotle, called the Golden Mean; that healthy state that lies between two extremes. Organizations which function within the Golden Mean or Gold Zone are people-centric. They highly value their people and it shows, but they also have healthy boundaries that let their people know what is expected of them. They clearly convey the benefits of working within the company's boundaries and the consequences of failing to, and they are dependably consistent in applying the benefits and consequences to every person in the company. Being performance-driven means that they reward performance and productivity rather than position or tenure. Employees of companies that function within the gold zone agree that it is one of structured freedom, and they express great appreciation for both the freedom and the structure.

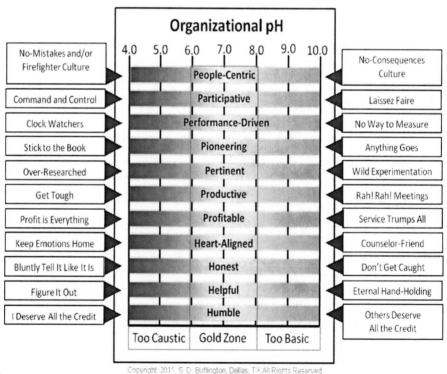

Illustration 8.1

The Disney model passes the Litmus Test and provides ample proof that adopting such a model would be a good move for companies of all kinds. According to multiple sources, the Disney organization is highly respected and highly profitable even years after the death of Walt. Disney's exceptional entertainment experiences, widely diverse content, and unique skill in managing businesses in an integrated manner have led to sustained success for decades. In fiscal 2013, Disney delivered record revenue, net income, and earnings per share for the third year in a row. The Walt Disney Company has been recognized as one of the most reputable companies in America and in the world by *Forbes Magazine* (2006-2013); one of America's most admired companies by *Fortune Magazine* (2009-2013); one of the World's most respected companies by *Barron's* (2009-2013); one of the best places to launch a career by *Businessweek Magazine* (2006-2010); and as company of the year by Yahoo Finance (2013).

The Disney company is highly people-centric and always has been. It has also always been highly structured, as any production company must be to pull off grand productions. Disney's employees are referred to as "cast members" and the people they serve are seen as their "guests." There is no question in anyone's mind what this relationship looks like. There are "off-stage cast members" and "on-stage cast members" and each knows their role precisely. There are both intrinsic and extrinsic rewards everyone shares in. The intrinsic rewards are happy "guests," a fun environment in which to work, a lot of freedom and flexibility, and the enjoyment that comes from being a cast member in a grand production. It's a bigger than life environment that fuels the imagination and feeds motivation.

Disney was highly participative and he built an organizational structure which promoted the continuance of that model: fun and freedom within clearly defined boundaries. He also made sure the structure was performance driven. Disney had a reputation for giving teams the challenge of coming up with "the best idea ever" and then bringing the teams together to collectively decide which team's idea was best. Once the best idea was selected, he would then ask the teams to find a way to "plus it." In time, the question on every cast member's mind was, "how can I come up with a really brilliant idea and, if my idea is selected, how can I plus it?" Imagine your company full of people thinking that way.

There is no question that Disney was a pioneer. He completely changed the face of entertainment and the approach to theme parks. And, as technology has provided greater and greater latitude in creating entertainment experiences, the Disney Company has been right on the cutting edge.

Disney's contribution is pertinent to employees who want a joyful place to work, to families who want a memorable experience, and to people who just want to forget life's struggles and escape into an amazing fantasy world for awhile. And, as the company's revenue, net income, and earnings per share reports show, there is no question this is a profitable strategy.

We use the term "heart-*aligned*" rather than heart-*centered* on the Corporate Litmus Test because heart-centered companies tend to lean toward the "base" end of the spectrum where employees are too loosely managed. Heart-aligned companies have a healthy balance between head and heart. Their policies consider and allow feelings in the workplace and keep them well balanced with structure and logic. Heart-aligned leaders realize that people are feeling creatures and that passion and motivation come through the feeling function. However, these healthy leaders don't move into the counseling and hand-holding space that takes up so much of a manager's time and energy in less healthy companies.

The Disney Company as it exists today is probably not perfect, but the model Walt Disney created is an enduring one that closely aligns with the values of the emerging workforce and with key factors for success so it is certainly worth examining.

Our Corporate Litmus Test provides another great model to follow. The goal there is to determine where your organization is now and to take speficic steps to get it into the Gold Zone.

Because we are committed to helping build highly engaged, high performance workforces and *guarantee* our work, the only way we can succeed is to meet our own standards, deliver everything we promise and then "plus it." We do that by working with clients who are as committed to positive change as we are. The Corporate Litmus Test provides us and our clients with clear guidelines that keep us all tracking successfully and that's what any good model should do.

CHAPTER NINE
There's a New Kid in Town

Between 2010 and 2014 six governments were overthrown (Egypt twice), six more were forced into change by citizen protests and civil disorder, five were experiencing ongoing major protests, at least five more were experiencing minor protests and several countries were in the midst of ongoing civil wars.

What is driving global unrest? In general, it's that third power shift which has given the newer generations a global view, a huge degree of transparency, the ability to communicate what they discover instantly, and the power of a global audience.

Before people could see the world in real time, most people had no idea whether their circumstances were good or bad; typical of what most people were experiencing or quite different. They had no idea how much money and privilege the elite had compared to them or what privileges they were being denied. Today they do know and they are greatly dissatisfied with the huge gaps they are finding.

The general consensus is that the unrest is being driven by dissatisfaction with the rule of local governments, wide gaps in income levels, dictatorial governance, human rights violations, concentration of wealth in the hands of autocrats, educated people without jobs, high unemployment, poverty, and the disparities these conditions create. Not surprisingly, these are the same things Millennials rankle against in many of America's large organizations, from Washington to Wall Street and beyond.

Many organizations report frustration when young employees just walk out the door as often occurs with Millennials when they observe organizational inequalities or injustice, and many of them don't stop there. They make sure the world knows what they have observed or experienced through websites like Glassdoor or Facebook. Some even actively sabotage their employer before they leave; 18% in the United States and 24% globally, according to recent *Gallup* polls.

If the new generations have the knowledge, awareness, drive and determination to destabilize or topple governments they are unhappy with, imagine what they can do to companies, no matter what the size. This is not some small change leaders can just ride out, it's an undeniable global force that must be acknowledged and managed. Those who don't manage it will drown in denial.

The tactics the newer generations are using to make massive changes on a global level include civil disobedience, civil resistance, defection, demonstrations, insurgency, internet activism, protests, revolution, riots, sit-ins, strikes, urban warfare and uprisings, to name a few. In the United States, "defection" or walking out the door, internet activism, protests, demonstrations, and strikes seem to be the preferred actions, but even those more civil actions can be devastating over the long haul. Organizations which remain blind to this global trend are likely to see an escalation of disengagement and push-back tactics.

The big cost for most organizations will not be active sabotage though. It will be disengaged employees who keep showing up and collecting a paycheck without contributing anything of real value to the organization.

A New Set of Lenses

1. The Generational Lens

Previous generations separated work from life. They were willing to endure less than ideal conditions at work to afford the lifestyle they wanted while away from work. That is not true of the two newest generations; Generation X and Millennials. To these generations earning a living must fit into their view of life.

Life for these generations was both protected and scary. The world at large offered no guarantees, yet their parents protected and, in many cases, even coddled them. They were given a voice and the right to make choices very early in life. Their relationships with their parents were collaborative and close to equal. In some cases, the child even held the dominant role. They grew up in a world of instant communication and immediate access to information. What all this led to was a generation of people who expect equality, consideration and instant access to everything. And when they don't get it, there is trouble in paradise, and this extends far and wide.

An example of the expectation of instant access is the ICMPA study, *24 Hours: Unplugged*. Based on research, the University of Maryland concluded that most college students are not just unwilling, but functionally unable to be without their media links to the world. The study asked 200 students at the College Park campus to give up all media for 24 hours. After their 24 hours of abstinence, the students were then asked to blog on private class websites about their experiences: to report their successes and admit to any failures. The 200 students wrote more than 110,000 words: in aggregate, about the same number of words as a 400-page novel.

"We were surprised by how many students admitted that they were 'incredibly addicted' to media," noted the project director Susan D. Moeller, a journalism professor at the University of Maryland and the director of the International Center for Media and the Public Agenda which conducted the study. "But we noticed that what they wrote at length about was how they hated losing their personal connections. Going without media meant, in their world, going without their friends and family." Bottom line: Without digital ties, students feel unconnected even to those who are close by. This experiment has been repeated each year since 2010 and has spread to a wider audience. In 2014 nearly 95% of Millennials said they were unwilling to go without their electronic connections for even 24 hours (Bart, 2010).

Another example of their insistence on instant results is what many professors are observing in Millennial students. What Traditionalists see as "cheating," Millennials see as collaboration. They see no value in spending hours poring through books when they can find the answers they are looking for instantly on the internet or by consulting with friends who have already found the answers. They have been using these strategies since they were children. There are "cheat books" on the internet that show them how to navigate through games without having to waste time figuring things out the hard way. They don't see this as cheating or breaking the rules. They see it as working smart rather than hard.

This unstructured, informal, situational approach seems perfectly natural to these generations and they have lots of evidence for its efficacy.

Look at game shows such as *Who Wants to Be a Millionaire* or *Cash Cab* where many "lifelines" are provided to reduce risk and increase the odds of winning. Contrast that approach against older game shows such as *Jeopardy, The Price Is Right,* or *Wheel of Fortune* where there is no help and you are on your own. To Gen Xers and Millennials the internet and the many forms of technology they use is a lifeline and they use it in ways few leaders understand.

An article in the *Harvard Business Review* explained the apparent opposition of the newer generations to following established rules this way, "Compared with their parents, young people are rule morphers; applying rules and conventions when convenient but changing or ignoring them when necessary. This carries over to work style and ethics, where young people tend to be informal and situational and much less structured than older generations (Dychtwald, Erickson and Morison 2006).

An example of how lack of understanding of the needs of this generation can wreak havoc is Michael Kramer, JC Penney's chief operating officer in 2012, who revealed to the *Wall Street Journal* that more than 30 percent of the bandwidth of JC Penney headquarters had been used for viewing YouTube videos during that month alone. Kramer consequently terminated 1600 employees in an effort to change the company's workplace culture (The Huffington Post, September 2013)

Whether there was an exploration into what employees were spending time on was not reported, but considering how the newer generations use technology, it is certainly possible that they were doing research rather than goofing off on company time. Perhaps they were trying to discover what the younger generations wanted so they knew how to help make the proposed product and image shifts that were being pushed out to the public. From what was reported, leaders just assumed the employees were wasting time entertaining themselves. Did anyone check before 1600 people got fired? Whether they did or didn't, a bigger question is, how did the firings alter the attitudes of the remaining employees? Based on the trajectory JC Penney was taking at the time, it appears the impact was not too beneficial.

Millennials have a very high sense of justice and readily react to things they consider unfair or extreme, so it's possible that many promising young employees walked out the door, literally or figuratuvely, with those who got fired.

Gen Xer's and Millennials tend to use technology in ways no other generation has. Not understanding their way of conducting business is costing organizations, and even entire industries, plenty. Most people, and certainly most businesses, mightily resist massive changes. They hold onto the old ways until it is painfully apparent that change is inevitable, at which point, the locked-in attitude shifts and possibility thinking begins to emerge.

The music industry is a prime case study in how technology coupled with the new mindset of the younger generations forced a well-established, but moribund business model into a period of punctuated equilibrium. That is, into an unplanned evolution where periods of relative stability were punctuated with bursts of rapid change. When the new generations began using the internet to download and share music, everyone in the traditional music system screamed, threw fits and pressed legal action over file sharing and streaming audio. This battle continued for years until reality finally set in and the industry realized things were not going to go back to the old ways.

According to music critic, Greg Kot, the music industry panicked when they discovered the approach of the new generations, and Kot observed that their panic was justified. Although new technology meant that more people than ever were listening to music, it also meant that record companies were no longer in full control. The internet made it easy for artists to market to their fans directly and for fans to acquire music free through file sharing. According to Kot "by some music business estimates, for every music file that is purchased online, 40 are shared (or 'stolen,' if you prefer to use the industry's parlance). Music itself is alive and well, even if the music industry as it once existed is not. Once, a handful of big corporations funneled heavily marketed recordings by superstar artists through a few radio chains and MTV to the public. Today, in place of that top-heavy business model, a new, brand of self-marketing is emerging, fueled by tweets, text messages and MP3 files" (Kot 2009).

The point here is, no matter how desirable a product or service is, the people who make them, sell them and buy them are not going to comply with rules they don't think are smart or useful. Organizations that try to control generational behaviors will only find themselves embroiled in greater and greater chaos dealing with more and more stress.

That's what happened in the music industry and what is happening in most corporations today.

Like those in the music industry, once businesses can see and accept the inevitability of the shift that is occurring right now, they can develop optimal new strategies and businesses will begin to evolve. Organizations that refuse to change will eventually disappear altogether. It's happening in the music industry now. According to Christopher Knab of *Fourfront Media & Music*, thirty years ago there were over 200 record distributors. Today there is only a handful (Knab 2008).

New generations are not going to give up the services or products they love, but they *are* going to change how they go about getting those products and services. They are not going to stop needing a job to support their lifestyle, but they *are* going to change how they work. Companies that want to survive and thrive into the future are going to have to do what the survivors in the music industry did; make major adjustments to the way they do business.

To understand the dynamic, it helps to examine industries which, in the past, were relatively stable (like the music industry) until a combination of technology and new generation thinking forced major changes. Major change is almost always stressful and increasing stress beyond healthy, motivational levels invariably increases vigilance, which leads to a locked-in attitude where change is strongly resisted. The result is escalating stress, chaos and lost profits, which eventually forces the industry to rethink their position. This creates break-over point where innovation replaces resistance and new ways to remain viable become the quest.

Increasing stress and chaos are plaguing many organizations today, and most are yet to hit that break-over point. People who were part of the stable past feel threatened and adopt a locked-in stance to protect and preserve the system they believe works. Their resistance increases stress and, to protect themselves, they disengage. Eventually, the stress and resistance will become so great that organizations will be forced to acknowledge the futility of trying to preserve past systems. Only then will a break-over occur.

Extreme stress occurs where there is the perception of a threat and, where a threat is perceived, all people—even leaders who can generally manage their emotions and actions well—unconsciously move into a protective stance. It's the old fight, flight or freeze fear response we are all so familiar with. When stress reaches peak levels in an organization, some people go into fight mode and get difficult; some go into flight mode and jump ship, and some freeze. Those who freeze may show up, but they aren't getting much done. Their brains are disengaged and they are essentially just riding out the time-clock. No organization is sustainable under such circumstances. It must eventually reach that break-over point where it begins making the necessary changes or it dies.

As demonstrated in *illustration 9.1*, during the resistance phase of catalytic change, stress and instability increase dramatically before stability is regained. A common response to this phase is to dig in and hold firm (lock in), which is what many organizational leaders are doing right now. Being aware that increased instability occurs at a critical break-over point can help leaders manage the chaos that often accompanies radical change and prepare to move through it more purposefully and strategically. Generally, catalytic change is a very slow process because stability does not reoccur until the majority has accepted the change and settled into it.

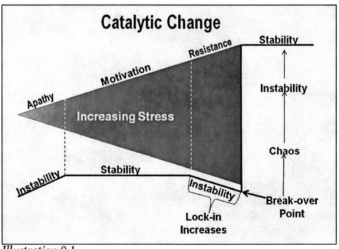

Illustration 9.1

According to *Rogers Innovation Adoption Curve* (*illustration 9.2*), only 2.5% of any population falls into the category of innovators. That appears to apply to business and politics as well as individuals. In spite of the fact that innovative companies, such as Apple, Amazon, Google, and Costco, are experiencing record profits and a continual climb to success, the older, more staid companies are holding firm. Even clear indicators showing the financial benefit of change, doesn't move the laggards off dead-center.

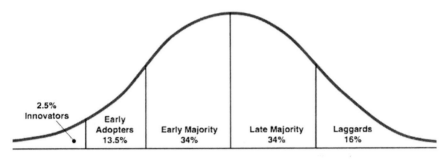

Rogers Innovation Adoption Curve

Illustration 9.2

Well-established Walmart, for example, appears to fall into the laggard category. The company is holding firm to the model they have used for years where the newer, fresher, employee-centric Costco, clearly an innovator, is doing things quite differently and prospering as a result. According to reports on the two companies, Costco reported a healthy 8% annual growth over five years where Walmart reported only 1.2 percent in the same period.

Walmart experienced a significant drop in sales which they blamed on the economy, yet during the same period, in an identical economy and selling to essentially the same customer base, Costco's profits were almost seven times that of Walmart in spite of the fact (and perhaps because of it) that Costco paid its employees almost double what Walmart did and provided more generous perks. Additionally, Costco enjoys markedly lower worker turnover and far higher sales per employee than Walmart. Costco averages an employee turnover rate of about 5 percent; far lower than Walmart. Costco's sales per employee figures are nearly double that of Sam's Club employees, which suggests that Costco employees are far more engaged in their work as well.

Walmart analysts could look at Costco's results and realize what needs to be done, but like many old, staid organizations, Walmart leaders cling to what once worked and resist substantial change. Public opinion and employee pushback forced Walmart to re-evaluate their position on employee salaries in 2015. Whether increasing salaries will be enough remains to be seen, but it appears Walmart executives finally hit the break-over point and are now at least exploring different options.

Unfortunately, the entrenched thinking that kept Walmart stuck for so long is all too common. In a *New York Times* article, author Tony Schwartz observed, "For most of us, in short, work is a depleting, dispiriting experience, and in some obvious ways, it's getting worse" (Schwartz 2014). This is a problem that needs to be addressed, and soon.

Several questions beg to be answered: What level of pain do most companies need to experience before they look at alternate strategies for growth and leadership? What will prompt struggling companies to invest more in their employees? How late into the game will the late majority and laggards be before they realize radical change is inevitable and begin making the necessary adjustments? Will they be able to recover at that point?

When the radically different core values of a large cohort forces change, instability increases for all but the innovators and early adopters who jump on that new wave early. Overall stability occurs only when late adopters finally accept the changes driven by innovators and early adopters, and begin adapting to the new reality. When change becomes a necessity and occurs late in the game, as is generally the case for the late majority and laggards, trying to catch up is a monumental task; one many such organizations may not be up to. The late majority and laggards make up a total of 50% of the population on the Rogers curve. They will eventually be forced to get on board or become obsolete. Until they do, the marketplace and the economy will continue to experience unstable conditions.

The early majority is actively looking for ways to make the shift and helping them do that is vitally important. Essentially, economic stability lies in the hands of the early majority (34% of the population) because they create the conditions that allow the late majority to get on board. The early majority doesn't lack the desire to change. If they aren't making change successfully, generally it's because they are still trying to tweak the old model and don't understand why that isn't producing the changes they desire. That's why early adopter organizations are what we focus on. We have found that once innovative early adopters know what to do they are quick to take action and can make the shift successfully.

Most change initiatives focus on the wrong things. Organizations spend a lot of time and money on procedures, processes and strategies they believe will help their people move through change more effectively, and this seldom works. There are organizations that have invested millions of dollars and many years on externally focused initiatives that have actually backfired or had a long-term negative effect. Because they get more and more expensive to maintain, externally driven change initiatives are often abandoned which leaves employees disillusioned and even more disengaged. For change to be successful, the first order of business has to be getting employees engaged and that means identifying and focusing on intrinsic motivators. We focus first and foremost on intrinsic factors in the work we do with clients because intrinsic motivation is what drives successful change.

When Will They Grow Up?

Managers frequently ask "When will the Millennials change?" or "When will they grow up and start behaving more like 'normal' people?" The answer is, and will continue to be, *never* in the way those asking mean since core values, which drive behaviors, rarely if ever change. The newer generations will grow up at about the same rate every generation has, but maturity only tones down idealistic dreams, it doesn't change core values. The values Millennials hold today are the values the vast majority of them will hold for life. Those values are truly an irresistible force which will continue to shape societies, businesses, entire industries (as occurred in the music industry) and, in time, world governments.

For more than a decade now a few insightful leaders have recognized and attempted to convey the benefits and strengths young workers bring to the workplace. They are quick learners, for example. They are adaptable and creative. They are independent thinkers who are technically savvy. They have a lot to offer the right employer.

Unfortunately, for every employer that sees and appreciates the strengths of the newer generations right now, there are a ninety-five who don't. Unenlightened managers keep waiting for these generations to "grow up" and be different, and it won't happen. Most leaders don't want to hear this, but it's the truth. The New Kids are not about to change. If you want to get the best from them, you must learn to adapt.

The stereotypical generalizations which are so frequently presented around Generation X and Millennials are what often prevent effective adaption on the part of leaders. Don't buy into them. To do so will prevent you from seeing their truth and tapping into their quite substantial strengths.

So what do the New Kids want? What must we know about them to better understand them and meet them where they live? And we *must* meet them where they live to remain viable in a world soon to be dominated by Millennials. Let's look at some of the typical views about Millennials and then at the reality. It's time to get to know the New Kid in town.

- **Typical View:** "They don't want to pay their dues. They expect to become president overnight."

- **Reality:** They don't really want the boss' job, just his or her respect and consideration. They want to contribute in meaningful ways, not just work in the background. They are collaborative and want a relationship with their coworkers, including the boss. They are smart and have learned to self-manage over the years so they resist those who try to manage them in ways that deny them the right to self-manage. They don't have a problem with structure. They want and expect that. But they have a big problem with lack of consideration and those who try to curtail their freedom to think for themselves.

- **Typical View:** "They have no work ethic."

  Reality: Millennials are dedicated to causes, not processes. They are more attracted to finding meaning and purpose than to just climbing a corporate ladder. Give them a reason to care about the work you want them to do and collaborate with them as they step into it and they will apply themselves to the job with great enthusiasm. You are never going to get them to care about processes. Fire them up around a purpose, however, and you won't need to keep motivating them. They will motivate themselves.

- **Typical View:** "They don't want to put in the hours to get the job done."

Reality: Tell this to Google or Facebook or Zappos or any of the other businesses that know how to manage the younger generations and they will promptly disprove this theory. Millennials don't mind long hours as long as they get to choose how, where and when they invest them, and as long as the hours they put in feel meaningful. They don't work for a paycheck. They work for a *cause*.

- **Typical View:** "They are not loyal. They just walk out the door without warning and never come back."

  Reality: There is some truth to this, but there are reasons for this response that need to be understood to prevent it from continuing to repeat. The newer generations firmly believe that their careers belong to them (not their employers). They value knowledge, continual improvement of skills, and an enjoyable work experience more than money or tenure. They prefer collaboration and resist hierarchies and work that feels meaningless, and they are quick to walk away from situations where they see little purpose or meaning or where they are not learning and growing on both personal and professional levels. If you want to keep the New Kids, you will need to be sure your workplace is fair, collaborative, meaningful, and a source of continual growth.

- **Typical View:** "They are totally self-absorbed."

  Reality: While it's true that Millennials really like themselves and enjoy sharing thier experiences through "selfies" and Facebook posts, they are the most altruistic generation in recorded history. They volunteer more and are more willing to risk everything for the common good than any generation since American Revolutionaries who established the United States Constitution. They seem self-absorbed because they see much of what passes for business and politics as meaningless and even harmful and are unwilling to compromise their deeply held values to play those games. They are still young and many may lack social graces, but they don't lack caring or commitment to things they believe in.

- **Typical View:** "They expect the company and everyone in it to bow to their desires."

Reality: This is not true. The fact that they refuse to play by the old rules, doesn't actually translate into expecting others to bow to their desires. What is typically happening is that older, more experienced employers and leaders have a set of expectations which the new generations don't buy into. This lack of compliance with the old, established rules can certainly seem like stubbornness or wanting one's own way, but in the mind of the Millennial they are standing up for what they believe is right and just, not just for themselves, but for all people. They can be great team players and tireless workers when their work is perceived as having purpose and meaning, not just to them, but to the world at large.

- **Typical View:** "They are not good at communication, and they are terrible at writing and spelling because they shortcut everything."

  Reality: While the propensity of these generations to shortcut communications with "text talk" is prolific, most of them had the same schooling older generations had. Like every generation before them, they learned to read, write and spell and, like all other generations, some do it better than others. They are very much about doing things faster and easier, and texting shortcuts are a way to do that. Where necessary, they can speak, spell, and communicate about as well as anyone. Their tendency to do things the quick, easy way is a product of growing up with the internet, and is actually highly useful in the fast-paced world we live in, and in which businesses function today. Text talk may be the shorthand of the future. Perhaps leaders should start learning it.

- **Typical View:** "They are overly dependent on their parents. They call them a thousand times a day."

  Reality: Maintaining strong personal connections with family and friends is extremely important to the Millennials. They are accustomed to connecting through technology and use it as a lifeline. Their gadgets keep them connected and help them collaborate. Their desire to connect and collaborate includes their parents.

The close relationship many Millennials have with their parents and the constant contact can be a good thing or a bad one depending on the parents and the kind of parenting the Millennial received. Parents who encourage independence and exploration, and who refuse to become crutches, generally act more as advisors and can provide great benefit to their grown children.

One of the marks of Millennials is that they don't want to do something the hard way when there's a faster, easier way to do it, and collaborating with more experienced advisors is an effective way to do that. Millennials who have healthy parents have a great resource. They can get better results faster and easier by consulting with their older, wiser parents. Good parents are also a source of support when the work environment doesn't support collaboration. The workplaces of Millennials in this group are actually positively impacted by parental support. It's like having the mind and experience of a seasoned adult (the parents) along with the quickness and agility of a young body (the Millennial).

It's a completely different story for Millennials with parents who don't know when to cut the cord or who are manipulative or controlling. This group becomes overly enmeshed and can't make a move without consulting their parents. In this case, the impact on the workplace can be quite negative. These Millennials can waste a great deal of time and drain off a lot of energy because the pipeline to mom or dad tends to be more gripe-fests than tapping into wisdom and experience for advice.

- **Typical View:** "They have an infinitesimal attention span."

  Reality: The newer generations grew up in an "A.D.H.D." world where things change quickly and everything happens fast. They have adjusted to this pace and have done a really good job of it. They actually have amazing powers of concentration when they choose to use them. They can sit down and play highly complex video games or build computer programs, or do anything else that deeply interests them for hours at a time. They can learn new computer programs and have them humming along in no time. They will spend hours learning all the features of their new cell phone or electronic pad so they can use them fully and efficiently. These abilities hardly point to an infinitesimal attention span. What it does point to is the the growing need for matching employees to jobs that truly interest them. You will never get Millennials to stay in a job because they need the money. They stay in a job and attend to tasks closely only when the work interests them.

Typical View: "They are social media obsessed."

Reality: Most Millennials expect to manage their own information and communication. According to an extensive study reported on in *The Millennial Index*, only a minority of Millennials (41%) spend more than three hours a week on Facebook and only 29% send more than three hours on YouTube. Twitter use is even less. Just 15% spend more than three hours a week on Twitter and 43% don't use Twitter at all. For those who do spend a lot of time online, they are not all busy organizing their social lives. The study found that Millennials spend far more time on work and study-related online forums and user groups than on social sites. They use technology frequently to connect with one another, which is what causes many to believe, mistakenly, that the younger generations are less effective socially than previous generations. They aren't. As with so many other things, they just socialize *differently*; through technology. Given their technological proficiency, they appreciate up-to-date technology in the workplace and most are well prepared to keep organizations humming in the age of technology. (*themillennialIndex.com/myths*)

- **Typical View:** "They don't follow rules."

Reality: Millennials rewrite, rather than reject rules in an effort to move things in a more positive direction. They have the tools to create, edit and shape their world in ways no generation before them has had. They prefer to keep their time and commitments flexible, and rules hinder flexibility; especially rules that make no sense to them, such as the rule that says you need to learn something new from a prescribed text book when the internet or collaborating with someone who already has the answer is so much faster and easier. Millennials are happy to apply rules that make sense and will move things forward. Technology is full of rules which they are able and willing to follow. Just don't expect them to follow mindless rules that have no direct application to what they are trying to accomplish.

- **Typical View:** "They are not interested in their work."

   Reality: What motivated previous generations does not motivate the new generations, especially Millennials. Money and status are not their priorities; meaningful experiences are. They will work hard if they believe they are making a difference and are appreciated. They do enjoy personal attention, but don't we all? Millennials have no resistance to change and little aversion to failure as long as they are learning something they can use in the future. They are cooperative team players as long as the team feels collaborative and has a direction and purpose they can believe in. They are all about the collective and gravitate towards group activities and learning. They want to be heard. They want frequent and useful feedback. They want their work to fit in with other life commitments and pursuits. They want to connect with others, including their bosses, and they want to have mentoring type relationships that help them learn what they need to learn to navigate life and business successfully. Provide these and you will be delighted with how interested they can be.

The latchkey experiences of many Gen Xers and Millennials have helped them develop emotional and intellectual attributes that play well amid the demands of a volatile marketplace and business environment. A lot of today's young workers are unhappy and disengaged, not because of inexperience or inability to adjust to the workplace, but because they seek a *different kind* of workplace, a different kind of employment deal, and a different kind of employer than they frequently encounter. The new generations highly value a congenial workplace, a lot of opportunity to learn and grow, and an optimal mix of work and life experiences; yet less than 30% say that have these.

The core values of every generation have always been an irresistible force. There has never been a time when the rules of past generations have dramatically altered the mindset of the current generation. Even extreme measures, such as torture and death, Genghis Khan style, have not stopped the inexorable march of generations driven by core values.

The New Kids in town are here to stay and they represent the largest cohort in history. The have strong opinions and a lot of power born, not just of their sheer numbers, but of their willingness to walk away from systems that are not working. Leaders can learn to ride the monster wave Millennials are creating and go very far, very fast or they can resist it and get swamped. What you do is entirely up to you, but our hope is that you will learn to ride the wave early. Those who do it well will become the new global giants.

The Cultural Lens

Not all differences are generational. Some are cultural, and many of the cultural differences don't serve American enterprise. When Traditionalists were the majority of the workforce, cultural values in the United States didn't create conflict because everything was business as usual and no one questioned the rightness of the hierarchical model.

Today, we live in a global world and awareness of better models is creating problems few could have predicted even thirty years ago. Take the concepts around learning, for example. We have already covered generational examples; now let's explore a cultural one.

When Jim Stigler was still a graduate student at the University of Michigan, he went to Japan to research teaching methods and found himself sitting in the back row of a crowded fourth-grade math class. "The teacher was trying to teach the class how to draw three-dimensional cubes on paper," Stigler explains, "and one kid was just totally having trouble with it. His cube looked all cockeyed, so the teacher said to him, 'Why don't you go put yours on the board?' So right there I thought, 'That's interesting! He took the one who can't do it and told him to go and put it on the board.'"

Stigler knew that in American classrooms, it was usually the best kid in the class who was invited to the board. And so he watched with interest as the Japanese student dutifully came to the board and continued to draw misshapen cubes. Every few minutes, the teacher would ask the rest of the class whether the kid had gotten it right, and the class would look up from their work, and shake their heads no. And as the period progressed, Stigler noticed that he (Stigler) was getting more and more anxious. "I realized that I was sitting there starting to perspire," he says, "because I was really empathizing with this kid. I thought, 'This kid is going to break into tears!' But the kid didn't break into tears," Stigler says, "he continued to draw his cube with equanimity. And at the end of the class, he did make his cube look right! And the teacher said to the class, 'How does that look class?' And they all looked up and said, 'He did it!' And they broke into applause. The kid smiled a huge smile and sat down, clearly proud of himself."

Stigler is now a professor of psychology at UCLA who studies teaching and learning around the world, and he says it was this small experience that first got him thinking about how differently the East and West approach the experience of intellectual struggle. "I think that from very early ages we [in America] see struggle as an indicator that you're just not very smart," Stigler says. "It's a sign of low ability — people who are smart don't struggle, they just naturally get it, that's our folk theory; whereas in Asian cultures they tend to see struggle more as an opportunity.

In Eastern cultures, Stigler says, it's just assumed that struggle is a predictable part of the learning process. Everyone is expected to struggle in the process of learning, and so struggling becomes a chance for the student to show that he has what it takes intellectually and emotionally to resolve the problem by persisting through that struggle.

Stigler allows for the fact that there is a lot of cultural diversity within the East and West and that it's possible to point to counter-examples in each culture, but says that, for the most part, in Western cultures, intellectual struggle in school children, and in workplaces, is seen as an indicator of weakness, while in Eastern cultures it is not only tolerated, but is often used to measure emotional strength (Spiegel 2012).

The lessons we get in school generally transfer to the workplace. So, in the United States, those who struggle to learn a skill are seen as weak. They are teased, judged harshly, ostracized and even fired from their jobs. These are sure ways to destroy any interest the individual might have had in learning a new skill. Because such responses are so common as to be expected in most Western organizations, many people are reluctant to even try learning something new, and both individuals and organizations lose out as a result. Even if the individual has the capacity to learn, negative feedback during the learning process may dash interest and, as we have already seen in the Performance Platform model, to the degree interest is lacking, learning is ineffective.

Creating interest is not as difficult as many organizational leaders make it look. Consider IDEO, an international design firm and consultancy. It's a great example of cultural change that works. IDEO leaders realized that they needed engaged innovative people so they created a powerful culture of creativity by making *collaborative generosity* their norm. IDEO exemplifies a help-friendly organization. Renowned for its creative output, the firm encourages frequent collaboration. They survey their employees to ensure they are happy and they map out helping relationships. The result is a culture of mutual assistance where help comes from all organizational levels. Those considered most helpful are described by coworkers as the most trustworthy and accessible, rather than the most technically competent. At IDEO, not only is there no shame in asking for help, it's expected. Their "help friendly" culture provides psychological safety and promotes collaboration, cooperation, creativity, and far greater output than is the norm in most organizations (Amabile, Fisher and Pillemer 2014).

Collaboration, interrelational support and structured freedom is the winning formula, and the one the most innovative and effective organizations are adopting. Once this model is established it costs nothing to sustain and the benefits are immense. Employees have to be part of the change and they have to see the initiative as authentic and lasting for them to be willing to adopt it. Employee buy-in is the key to long-term success. Though the initial steps are not easy, the end result in performance, productivity and profits is well worth it.

The Meme Lens

The meme lens extends far beyond cultural differences to include globally held beliefs. As you may recall, memes are globally transmitted ideas, symbols, or practices that are conveyed through writing, speech, gestures, rituals or other imitable phenomena. Where a generational lens develops around the values of a cohort and a cultural lens develops around local customs and attitudes, memes develop around entire cultures and can span generations.

In chapter two we gave an overview of Spiral Dynamics which is a view of memes over time. We mentioned that most old line corporations and governments are still functioning within the power and control meme where general populations have moved far beyond that, which has created a wide gap. In *illustration 9.3* we see the progression from

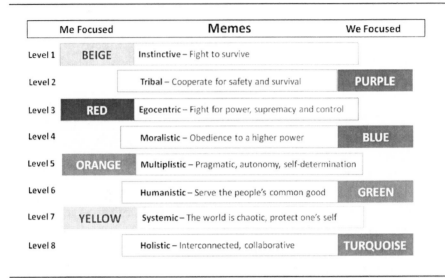

	Me Focused	Memes	We Focused
Level 1	BEIGE	Instinctive – Fight to survive	
Level 2		Tribal – Cooperate for safety and survival	PURPLE
Level 3	RED	Egocentric – Fight for power, supremacy and control	
Level 4		Moralistic – Obedience to a higher power	BLUE
Level 5	ORANGE	Multiplistic – Pragmatic, autonomy, self-determination	
Level 6		Humanistic – Serve the people's common good	GREEN
Level 7	YELLOW	Systemic – The world is chaotic, protect one's self	
Level 8		Holistic – Interconnected, collaborative	TURQUOISE

Illustration 9.3   *Adapted from Don Beck's Spiral Dynamics*

the *instinctive* survival concepts held by early humans, to the *tribal* mentality still seen in more primitive cultures, to the *egocentric* "might is right" mentality of kingdoms, feudal systems, most governments, and most old line businesses.

The exploitative nature of the egocentric, power structure organizations adopted was not lost on early religious institutions. They took advantage of this power position and upped the ante by attributing the right to power to a source even higher than man, creating the *moralistic* meme which still rules most religions around the world. Science and philosophy introduced new perspectives grounded in pragmatism which resulted in the *multiplistic* meme and introduced the idea of autonomy from ruling bodies. It was at this point that workers began to assert their rights and unions were born. Psychology and philosophy ushered in the *humanistic* era and rapid change led to the *systemic* view that protecting self was an essential part of life. The global reach of the internet has provided a view of how interconnected we all are and has led to the prevailing *holistic* view of the Millennial generation and of a large and growing group of people generally referred to as Cultural Creatives.

Traditionalists in Western cultures straddle the moralistic and multiplistic memes. Baby Boomers straddle the multiplistic and humanistic memes. Gen Xers adopted the systemic meme, and Millennials sit squarely in the middle of the holistic meme.

The command and control "might is right" mindset continues to be the model that is handed from one generation of leaders to another and few leaders have ever stepped back from this much touted model to ask if it still works. This model is five levels removed from the holistic Millennial meme and isn't working. Yet, it is so deeply entrenched that many businesses, some long established, have shriveled up and died rather than abandon this long outdated model. Where organizations are still functioning from a "life is a battleground" mentality, Millennials are functioning from an integrated, interactive, collaborative world view and the two are mutually exclusive. Millennials don't share the egocentric power view. They actively resist it, and their approach is to separate themselves from it mentally, emotionally and physically, which is proving very costly to organizations stuck in the past.

3. The Societal Lens

As any new generation enters the workforce, it brings along with it new technological ideas and new social norms which inevitably spawn change in societies and organizations of all kinds. The greater the generational differences, the more radical the change.

Young people have always been the innovators in any society, but they are also not yet as skilled or productive as their older counterparts. They are still experimenting, testing and creating. In the process, they throw out old rules and create new technologies and social revolutions. This makes the "changing of the guards" difficult and forces older, more mature industries and organizations into radical restructuring. This is happening today in epic proportions because one large and powerful generation, Baby Boomers, is now being forced to acquiesce to a new, larger and equally powerful generation, Millennials. Though they clash in the workplace and are in very different places in their lives, these two powerfully significant generations hold dear very similar values when it comes to personal freedom.

In their youth, Baby Boomers were the flower children and hippies who proudly decorated their clothing, their cars, and their lives with peace signs and happy faces. They took to the streets to protest the Vietnam War; they handed out flowers with wishes for "peace and love;"

and marched for causes they believed in as the Traditional generation looked on in disgust.

As Boomers got older and entered the world of work, they began to adopt the "be responsible employees" teachings of their Traditional parents and bosses. They stepped into the workplace and became responsible employees in the Traditional style. They sacrificed work-life balance where Millennials are not willing to do that. So Boomers look at the free-spirited Millennials and think, "I didn't get to do that; why should they?"

Every significant generational guard change, such as occurred when the Baby Boom generation took the reins and which is now occurring with the Millennial generation, seeds a growth cycle of powerful new organizations that dominate and direct the marketplace. Microsoft and Apple are examples of game-changers from the Baby Boom generation. Google and Facebook are examples of Millennial-driven game-changers.

Organizations that recognize the power behind a power shift and the direction in which it is shifting have a huge advantage for at least two generations into the future. The key trends driving the changes today are not the technological changes which drove the Baby Boom generation. For Millennials, technology is a given and is just a means to an end. The biggest trend now, and one every organization needs to prepare for, is the *social shift* from outer-directed to inner-directed behavior.

Outer-directed people are conformists. They look to systems and external cues to know where they fit, how to behave, and how to view life. Inner-directed people look to their own needs and desires. They measure their capacity not by the approval of others, but by their own perception of their strengths and limitations. Inner-directed people tend to be proactive in designing their lives, their work environment, and the products and services they use so these best suit their needs. Understanding the significance of the socially and informationally connected world of Millennials and their motivation is critical to riding the big wave of change that is now upon us.

Generational theorists, Neil Howe and William Strauss, suggest that there are four generational types which appear in cycles. They call the four types Idealistic, Reactive, Civic and Adaptive. According to this theory, an era starts with an Idealist generation which is focused on social issues and which question and challenge the morals of institutions.

Idealists are born and grow up in a more stable world where crime is low, optimism is high, and children are indulged.

The Idealist generation is followed by the Reactive generation This generation is born during a period of 'awakening' when society is focused on 'self' rather than community. Crime starts to rise and children are under-protected, which leads them to focus on pragmatic solutions and survival. Reactives are usually rebellious, independent, and cynical, and are usually branded as a "bad" generation.

Next, is the Civic generation which is focused on how to 'clean things up', and on finding consensus in a divisive 'unraveling' culture. They are geared toward rebuilding institutions. This generation values optimism and team-work.

Finally comes the Adaptive generation, a generation born during a societal 'crisis' such as we are experiencing now. This generation tends to be over-protected. They value sensitivity, fairness and cooperation, tend to be conformists, and are usually labeled as a "good" generation.

- **Baby Boomers** are considered **Idealists**
- **Gen Xers** are considered **Reactives**
- **Millennials** are considered **Civics**
- **Post-Millennials** are expected to be **Adaptives**
  (Howe and Strauss 2000)

The Lens Effect

Telescopes utilize the effect of gaps between stacked lenses to greatly magnify images. Organizational gaps tend to create the same magnifying effect, especially when the gaps exist on several levels. Leaders around the world, from governments to corporations, are trying to figure out how to minimize the ever-growing challenges they encounter. Few bother to look at the magnifying effect of the ever widening gaps between the lenses through which they view the world and those through which the general populations look.

Organizations still functioning from the egocentric power meme are never going to drag Millennials into their outdated world. To connect with them, organizations are going to have to meet Millennials where they live and right now that's quite a leap; a leap far greater than many leaders are willing to take.

Millennials are well aware of organizational reluctance to bridge that wide gap, and they are not waiting. The growing trend today is away from employer/employee relationships and toward subcontracting services to organizations. This may or may not be a beneficial transition for organizations, but they can expect it to continue and expand unless they make some radical changes.

Ricardo Semler of Semco says he prefers to hire subcontractors because it is a more effective utilization of people. He believes it taps into their natural drive for fulfillment, meaning, and engagement. "It's interesting what people can do," Semler says, "when a system for independence and meaningful work exists." (*Semler 1995*)

We find it interesting that, in spite of the fact that most people are perfectly capable of functioning on their own and even thriving outside of the workplace, leaders and managers think they need to be managed, controlled or worse yet, threatened, to function effectively once they enter the sacred halls of the corporation. The high performance workplaces of mavericks like Semler regularly prove that people are far more effective when given clear objectives and the opportunity to govern themselves as they achieve them.

In 2009 economist, Harry S. Dent, observed that "Corporations have nothing to fear but their own paranoia." That was a pretty accurate view before Millennials arrived on the scene. Paranoia is certainly something that needs to be eliminated, but today, there is more to fear than just paranoia. Leaders today need to fear the ever widening gap that, even with paranoia eliminated, won't come anywhere near closing until leaders learn to lead caringly, collaboratively and authentically. Millennials are unusually effective at detecting insincerity and feigned caring is summarily rejected. Once you lose their trust, getting it back is difficult, if not impossible.

The New Kid in town is here to stay and the game has changed dramatically. Leaders need to realize that the lenses they have been looking through for decades are clouded and no longer yield a clear view of the road ahead. There's a solution, but to get to it, you may need some new lenses.

CHAPTER TEN
Mindset and Energy

Ultimately, mindset is what drives or derails performance. Energy is what sustains it. Without the right mindset, training and development efforts are a waste of time and money, and without sustained energy, keeping yourself or your employees engaged is next to impossible.

The effect of mindset can be seen in Theories X, Y and Z management styles. Theory X managers create environments where people are tightly controlled and managers are taught to push for performance.

Theory Y managers create environments that give people a lot of latitude to perform, but that are often too lax when it comes to structure.

Theory Z managers create healthy, balanced environments where both they and their people thrive.

Because mindset drives energy in a particular direction, the beliefs theory X and Y leaders hold about people tend to create conditions where the environment is unhealthy and the response of employees to that environment perpetuate the leader's assumptions.

You find four kinds of environments in workplaces and only one of them is healthy. The other three create problems in one way or another. Each of the four environments is created and sustained by the mindset of the leader and, over time, the prevailing environment creates a culture that then drives the direction in which energy flows throughout the organization.

The organizational culture in turn determines the mindset of the people, and the mindset of the people determines the success or failure of the organization.

It all begins and ends with the mindset of the leader which is why the right kind of leadership development it is so vitally important to organizational success.

The Four Cultures are:

- **No Mistakes** (too rigid and overly structured – Theory X taken to extreme)
- **No Consequences** (too lax and unstructured – Theory Y taken to extreme)
- **Firefighter** (an odd combination of too unstructured in some places and too rigid in others – vacillation back and forth between Theories X and Y rather than balance)
- **Structured Freedom**^{tm} (a healthy environment in which clear boundaries and the freedom to function well within them avoids extremes – Theory Z)

In a No Mistakes environment, there are very strict rules to which everyone is expected to adhere. There is a time to show up to work, a time to take a break, a time to go home and a very detailed rulebook that no one is allowed to deviate from, even if the rules don't make a lot of sense. Many bureaucracies and governmentally run organizations function in this culture.

In a No Consequence environment, whatever rules exist are loosely adhered to and are inconsistently and unpredictably applied. In this culture no one knows what to expect. Slackers are given the same consideration as top performers and bullies are given free reign. As a result, the top performers generally get disgusted and leave which leaves only underperformers, increasing the cycle of ineffectiveness.

In a Firefighter environment, upper management dictates the results they want to a team manager and the team manager is held responsible for getting those results from their team. In a healthy environment this could be a good system, but in a Firefighter environment the structure that would allow the level of performance expected is not there so team managers end up trying to take up the slack by doing much of the work themselves. As a result much of the manager's time is occupied with task management and the people are left to figure things out on their own. Predictably, mistakes get made and projects fail to get completed on time and, when they do, the over-worked, short-tempered manager sees another fire to put out. Burnout is the inevitable outcome. In a Firefighter environment there is a lot of activity, but not a lot of productivity due to high chaos and very high levels of stress

In a healthy **Structured Freedom**^{tm} **environment,** boundaries are clear and there is no question what will happen when someone steps outside them. Yet, within those clear boundaries there is a lot of freedom and flexibility in how the job gets done. Employees in this kind of environment often describe their leader as providing them with the information, tools, and processes they need to do their job well and then trusting them to perform. They know there will be a reward for excellence and a consequence for poor performance or behavior, and they know exactly what that is. Almost all employees need structured freedom to perform at their best and almost all employees prefer it.

The Top Ten Reasons Employees Leave Companies

According to hedge fund manager and founder of Ironfire Capital, LLC, Eric Jackson, who manages funds for many large organizations, the top ten reasons why top performers leave an organization (Jackson 2011.

The ten reasons most frequently reported are:

1. **Big company bureaucracy.** This is the number one reason given in exit interviews. Bureaucracies are rife with rules that make no sense and complaints about the problems they create are generally ignored. Top performers won't continue to follow mindless rules.

2. **Lack of interest and passion for the job being done.** Most companies don't bother to ask employees if they are enjoying their current project or if they are really interested in the work they are doing. HR people are usually too busy keeping up with other things to bother and bosses are usually too tapped out on time. Whether an employee is interested in and enjoying their work is seen as a "nice to have" perk rather than a "must have" part of the job. Unless leaders see this as a "must have," they might as well kiss their best people goodbye. The emerging workforce is not driven by money and power. They want the opportunity to be a part of something meaningful.

3. **Poorly administered annual performance reviews.** Most companies do a very poor job of administering annual performance reviews, and most employees dislike them. Generally, performance reviews are rushed through, with a form quickly filled out and sent off to HR, so everyone can get back to "real work". The impression this leaves with the employee is that

their boss and, therefore, the company is not really interested in their daily activities or their long-term future. Most employees want and need feedback far more frequently, preferably in the moment as exemplary performance or poor performance occur so they can make meaningful adjustments in real time.

4. **Lack of career development planning.** Most employees don't know what they will, or should, be doing in 5 years. Less than 5% of people are able to answer that query. However, most employees want to explore what the future holds with their employer and want the help of their boss in planning it. This is not a discussion most managers even imagine having; not even with their top talent. This presents a huge opportunity for leaders who take the time to have such discussions. It lets employees know their employer thinks there is a path for them going forward which can be a big motivator.

5. **Shifting priorities.** Priorities will inevitably change as business needs shift, and giving employees new, exciting projects to work on can serve to keep them engaged. Change, in and of itself, is not the problem. Problems arise when priorities shift too quickly and there is no strategic plan for rearranging current priorities so everything continues to flow. When you commit to a project, be sure to give those responsible for getting it done enough time to complete it. If you have to change mid-stream for some reason, sit down with your employees and explain why the shift must occur.

6. **Lack of accountability.** When employees are not held accountable for bad behavior or lack of performance, top talent becomes disgusted and loses interest in performing for a leader or organization that accepts and allows such things. Many organizations keep people on the payroll that really shouldn't be there. When employers are asked why, they give a litany of rationales such as, "It's too hard to find a replacement" or "Now's not the time." Know that your best people are turned off by poor performers. If you want to keep your best people, make sure they are surrounded by other great people.

7. **Managers telling employees how to do their job.** Top talent demands accountability from others and they expect to be held accountable for their projects, but they don't need or appreciate

being told how to do their job. Have regular touch points with your people as they work through their projects, but let them decide how the project gets done.

8. **Vision is not conveyed**. Do your employees know what your company's vision is? Do they share this vision? Do they know what strategy you are executing or want to execute? Do they know what role they are to fill in this? Do they know *why* your company does what it does? If not, you have some work to do. Very few companies bother to convey their *why*. They think business is about making money, but that doesn't inspire dedication or engagement. A company's "why" needs to center around the purpose, cause or belief around which the company was formed; around what drove the founder to create the organization in the first place. Be sure to convey your "why" because that is what inspires performance. Performance is *not* driven by what you do and how you do it. When leaders communicate the purpose or cause of the organization, they literally tap into the part of the brain that inspires performance.

9. **Lack of open-mindedness/failure to listen.** Top performers have great ideas and want to share them, but many companies are too invested in established rules to hear or consider them. Some even view those with different ideas and suggestions as rogues who are not team players. When high performance people are not heard, they often get disgusted and leave. What the organization is left with then is a lot of "yes" people telling leaders just what they want to hear. That might keep those leaders happy, but it's all an illusion; a house of cards that will at some point come tumbling down. Listen to others' points of view and, where possible, incorporate the best suggestions.

10. **The boss**. If people under a particular boss quit or ask for transfers more frequently than usual, you should take a serious look at that manager. Sometimes they need to be moved to another position, but in many cases it's possible to help poor leaders improve significantly. Most people who aspire to lead have the right stuff, but having it and having it developed to effective levels are two different things. Leaders who have the right attributes can be quickly developed with the right training.

Ultimately companies that take such approaches have suffered, and will continue to suffer, the loss of good people because of outdated individual and organizational mindsets. Smart leaders are continually searching for better methods they can implement and are taking steps right now rather than waiting for a crisis to hit.

The successes of companies like IDEO, Netflix, and Google demonstrate the importance of creating people-friendly cultures. These companies have tossed out, or never adopted, the standard management playbooks and focus instead on creating trust and comittment. Common sense is the rule, and the dominant belief is that hiring people who align with and support a high performance workplace, and then giving them clear guidelines and plenty of freedom will result in a workforce where most employees will do the right thing. And, as it turns out, they do.

The Four Main Barriers to Greatness:

- Fear (often presents as short tempered irritation or anger)
- Erroneous beliefs (sustained because no one can see their own filters and blind spots)
- Lack of knowledge/skills
- Physical barriers (less than 5% of the cause)

These barriers affect the performance and results of leaders as well employees. In fact, the higher up the organization an employee goes, the more critical it is that the first three factors are managed, and that they are not the primary lenses through which the individual is looking.

If a leader is angry or fearful, for example, that leader's actions or failure to act will negatively impact the entire company. The same is true when actions are taken as a result of erroneous beliefs. In lower level employees those same factors would likely only affect their job or the team they work directly with. With a leader, the whole organization is impacted.

Strengths Versus Energizers

When it comes to hiring, placement, and development, most organizations focus on observable behaviors, learned skills, and measurable strengths. But strengths and energizers are two different things. Being effective at something you don't have any passion for or energy around creates proficiency traps which drain energy and lower the capacity to excel.

It is not uncommon to find people who are caught in a proficiency trap, and although such individuals have functional strength in that arena, they don't perform as effectively over the long haul as someone who actually enjoys the task because their lack of interest cannot sustain the behavior. Ultimately, unless people are doing what they love or what is natural to their authentic style, loss of interest and burnout are inevitable outcomes.

When burnout occurs and employers begin to notice effectiveness waning, they typically deal with it by (1) giving the employee a pep talk, (2) providing skills training, (3) giving a warning, (4) putting the employee on a performance improvement plan, (5) expressing concern and/or disappointment, and/or (6) firing them. The more enlightened leaders bring in a coach at some point, but if the coach doesn't know how to reignite interest and energy, that usually fails as well.

That's the downside. There are also situations where a leader sees a diamond in the rough, asks the right questions or hires a good coach who can bring out the brilliance in a high potential, and ends up with a star performer.

An example of this is a man who became an accountant, though he had no passion for that profession, because his dad was an accountant. Over time doing the work of an accountant became harder and harder and he asked to be reassigned to a sales position. Though he had no training or experience in selling, his boss was able to see his potential and gave him the opportunity to learn. In less than two years this man was the company's top salesperson.

Potentially great employees often get overlooked because their employers fail to consider that their performance on a particular job is not a measure of their *capacity* to perform. People in the wrong job never perform at their best, and making decisions based solely on performance in one area is a bad practice. When leaders are focused on *learned* skills and abilities rather than on *natural* skills, abilities, and interest, they are looking at surface measures. More often than not employees are under-performing, not because they are incapable of performing well, but because they are disinterested and disengaged for some reason

Almost everyone has the capacity to perform tasks that don't energize or motivate them for awhile and, since most employers focus primarily on skills, they hire people who have the skills the job requires already developed. That's a good practice as long as the skills align with natural strengths and abilities. When they don't, a new hire may perform well in the beginning, but perfomance will drop markedly when the inevitable burnout sets in.

Illustration 10.1 demonstrates the effect of learned skills when they are aligned with natural skills versus learned skills that are maintained out of fear or a sense of duty. When learned skills align with natural attributes, the result is ease of application, enjoyment, self-motivation, and the drive to keep growing and achieving. This natural drive results in practicing, polishing, and perfecting related skills, which leads to sustained excellence.

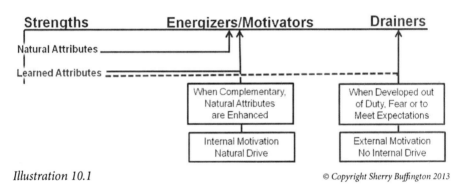

Illustration 10.1   © *Copyright Sherry Buffington 2013*

Learned strengths which are in opposition to natural attributes can be useful in helping us manage life's events, but if relied upon too heavily or for too long, they create resistance and drain energy. Where we are working against our nature, any appearance of motivation is driven by fear or a sense of duty, neither of which results in sustained high performance. Non-complementary learned attributes are draining and generally must be *externally* motivated.

Energy in the Workplace

Where vision, passion, and skills align, energy flows and star performers emerge. Steve Jobs is a great example of this. Though he had a reputation for being a tough leader, he was also a master at inspiring innovation and performance in his people. Those who knew Jobs, described him as tireless. That's the energizing effect of aligning skills to passion and vision.

Leaders who inspire people to star performance such as Jobs did, are not just good at conveying their vision, they also share their passion in a way that is contagious. When you examine great leaders, that contagious quality is always there. Leaders like Herb Kelleher, founder of Southwest Airlines; Richard Branson, founder of the Virgin empire; Ricardo Semler of Semco; Meg Whitman, Hewlett-Packard CEO; Larry Page and Sergeny Brin, co-founders of Google, Tony Hsieh, and founder of Zappos, all have that contagious quality in common. Not only are they tireless themselves, they inspire tireless dedication in others. The same was true of great leaders, such as the late Walt Disney and Sam Walton, who built empires that are still thriving

Energized employees are an organization's greatest asset, yet few organizations take steps to foster energizing environments. Far too many leaders mistake bravado for inspiration and wonder why, in spite of all their efforts, their people continue to function below their potential. Energizing people requires a deeper understanding of what drives and energizes them than those who are invested in bravado are willing to gain.

A good example of how leader bravado can adversely affect an entire team is Jerry Jones, the owner of the Dallas Cowboys. Jones is a shrewd businessman worth billions of dollars, but he is not a coach or general manager. Still, Jones insists on telling the top coaches he hires how to coach. The coaches generally deal with it for awhile, but micromanagement is an energy drainer and, in time, the coach's energy begins to wane and the whole team is affected.

Further down the Cowboys ladder are problematic players, such as was Terrell Owens. Overall, the antics of Jones are nowhere near as over the top as those of Owens, but Jones' impact has been far greater. In the overall scheme of things, the misadventures of Owens is little more than a blip on the radar screen, but according to team records, Jones' approach has cost the Dallas Cowboys many wins over the last 20 years and has taken the entire franchise off-course.

The overall record of the Dallas Cowboys since Jones took it over is .500 at best, which means the team has lost as many games as they have won. Prior to Jones buying the Dallas Cowboys in 1989, "America's

Team" was the only NFL team to record 20 straight winning seasons (1966-85), a period in which they only missed the playoffs twice. They won five Super Bowls before Jones bought the franchise, and three after, two of which were under Coach Jimmy Johnson, who it is reported was fired because he refused to coach the way Jones thought he should. Though the Dallas Cowboys franchise is still one of the highest valued in the world today, it has been twenty years since they have had a Super Bowl win and many sports franchises would view their .500 record as a failure.

A new coach may come along and bring the Dallas Cowboys back to their glory days, but that coach will need to be quite influential, not just with the players, but with Jones as well. Generally it takes an influential leader to open the eyes and mind of a superior who is on a destructive path. It can be done though. As consultants and business advisors, we have seen it happen many times.

We use Jerry Jones as an example because the Dallas Cowboys are highly visible and Jones' reputation is well known. Jones is not an anomaly. This same thing happens in companies across the nation and throughout the world tens of thousands of times every day. Leaders who make choices based on flawed beliefs and a closed mindset invariably have blind spots that can lead organizations awry.

Leaders don't intentionally drain off the energy of their followers, yet that is the effect many have. Generally, this occurs because they don't know their people or themselves well enough to be a positive influence. They unknowingly allow one or more of the main barriers to success— fear, erroneous beliefs and/or lack of knowledge/skills—to override their good intentions.

The primary difference between the leaders of highly profitable organizations and the leaders of stagnant or declining organizations is *mindset*, a product of beliefs, attitudes and emotional states. Because mindset is a fixed mental attitude or disposition that predetermines an individual's responses to, and interpretations of, situations, it directly affects performance on every level.

Leaders who have not harnessed their own mind and emotions are ineffective no matter how positive their intent, and the reason runs far deeper than most imagine. Unmanaged thoughts and emotions produce a great deal of stress, burn off a lot of energy and fuel a downward spiral of negative reactions.

According to a 2012 study of brain function conducted by Yale University, unmanaged thoughts and emotions can also affect brain function. Yale researchers found that grey matter in the pre-frontal cortex, the region of the brain that regulates emotions, desires and impulses, is measurably reduced by frequent or sustained stress. The indication is that being regularly exposed to stressful situations actually further impairs an individual's ability to control impulses and regulate emotions. This has huge implications for both leaders and their teams.

We regularly hear reports of leaders who throw temper tantrums, stonewall, publicly embarrass their employees, yell, scream, and act in a host of other wholly unproductive ways. Generally, these out of control executives avoid anything that might require introspection and they don't bother to get to know their people on any meaningful level. They are deeply invested in external shows of success and they prefer to have the spotlight shining in their direction. Though they may have read all the right books on leadership, they are unable to get out of their own way. They seek to manage or control the behaviors of their people rather than lead them, which produces resistance and backlashes that make matters worse and increase stress. As stress goes up, the ability to think clearly drops creating an ever worsening cycle of ineffectiveness for everyone.

External focus and insufficient awareness of employee wants and needs creates conditions where true motivation cannot even be effectively implemented, much less sustained. Abraham Maslow's Hierarchy of Needs helps to explain why efforts at motivation fail when leaders are externally focused.

The first two levels on Maslow's hierarchy, physiological survival needs and safety, (*Illustration 10.2*) are externally driven. Energy expended at these levels is easily depleted so efforts to fulfill these needs are abandoned as soon as the need is met. As a result, motivation is sporadic, unpredictable and temporary at best.

The leader types we call Enforcers and Abdicators attempt to manage and motivate employees from these two need levels. Enforcers rely on extrinsic rewards, threats of punishment, manipulation, and power plays in an effort to improve performance.

Abdicators don't push the way Enforcers do. They believe people work to meet these two basic needs and assume the money and perks the job provides will be enough to keep employees motivated. Money and perks are rarely prime motivators, and using them to drive performance can get very expensive. When Abdicators need to press people into action, they are more inclined to use guilt or shame than force. Both approaches keep people stuck in the first two high effort/ low energy levels which are doomed to fail eventually.

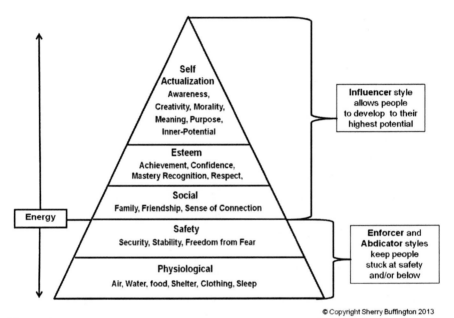

© Copyright Sherry Buffington 2013

Illustration 10.2

The levels above safety—social, esteem and self-actualization—are self-driving intrinsic motivators that are self-perpetuating. These levels are frightening to Enforcers and Abdicators because they assume giving people this much power will usurp their own power and cause them to lose control.

Influencers have a very different mindset. They know that *intrinsic* motivation increases dedication and drive, and that it doesn't have to be artificially induced. They know their people and realize the power of the social, esteem, and self-actualization levels to increase energy, interest, and engagement, and drive performance. Influencers inspire people to reach for the stars; to keep developing toward their highest potential. They realize that command and control tactics simply teach people to wait to be told what to do rather than taking the initiative to get an outcome so they never employ those tactics. They understand the importance of trust and a sense of belonging, and promote a feeling of "family" in the workplace. The feeling that they are part of a family that really does care about them is a very prominent quality among employees in successful companies. Employees who feel understood and supported happily serve their company, their leader, their coworkers, and customers. In such an environment productivity is high and employee turnover low. This sense of belonging is the glue that holds teams together and creates high performance workplaces.

We see a much higher level of commitment and a greater number of high performers in companies where leaders empower their people and foster a sense of belonging. An example is a family-oriented franchisee client of ours. In interviews with their top performers, feeling that they were part of a family and that their leader had their back (trust) were the two most frequently mentioned factors for why they were willing to do whatever it took to get great results. Moreover, all reported high levels of satisfaction and no intention of ever leaving their employer.

About a year after our interviews, the franchisor rearranged its structure and, in the process, the franchisee lost some of its stores to the franchisor and inherited others that were once managed by the franchisor. Where the franchisee provided a family culture, the parent company emphasized numbers and results with little personal concern for people and, within months, some of the top producers who had been with the franchisee for years left the parent organization because the sense of belonging was gone, and got in line to be rehired by the franchisee when a store became available.

On the flip side, the energy and attitudes of the managers of the corporate stores which were absorbed by the franchisee into the family culture shifted up dramatically and the performance of those managers greatly improved. None of these managers wanted to return to the parent company.

The stores didn't change. Neither did the duties, the marketplace or the product line. What did change was the leadership style and the environment it fostered.

Transparency, Meaning and Purpose

Part of a healthy family-like culture is transparency and the ability to convey something more than rules and expectations. Employees are motivated by things that have meaning and purpose and by believing that can trust their leader. Many leaders are uncomfortable with transparency, but it is consistently named as a key factor for developing trust. People want to know the story behind the organization they work for. They want to know the heart and soul of it as well as the body. Most companies only reveal the body: procedures, systems, strategies for success, expectations, and rules. Great leaders show and share the heart and soul of the company as well as the body.

We hear a lot about work/life balance these days and many leaders assume this is about balancing time at work with time off the job, but that isn't what it's about at all. In researching the wants and needs of Gen Xers and Millennials, what we hear time and time again is that these generations are looking for what would essentially be described as a healthy home environment at work; a place where they are seen, heard and appreciated; a place where their thoughts, needs and ideas are valued; a place where they are helped to grow and develop rather than being controlled and limited. In short, a place that feels like a second home. They want their work to feel like an extension of family and friends. Employees in a work environment such as this actually spend more time at work than at home by choice.

One leader we interviewed reported that his employees enjoyed being at work so much that many of them didn't want to go home at the end of their shift. This leader owns pizza restaurants and 70% of his employees are Millennials. What makes this truly remarkable is that turnover is notoriously high in the fast food industry, and organizations the world over complain about how hard it is to keep Millennial employees. Yet turnover is almost non-existent at Nick's Pizza and Pub in Chicago. Nick has defied all odds and his company is now the sixth busiest independent pizza company in per-store sales in the United States, and is growing rapidly. The philosophy of Nick Sarillo, the founder and innovative leader, is that work should be purpose-driven and the workplace should be treated as a school in which everyone is always learning, growing and improving. This is music to Millennial ears.

Nick has created an innovative, compassionate, nurturing, supportive, ever evolving community in which his people feel very much at home, which is why no one wants to leave. His community is so transparent that everyone's salary, including Nick's, is posted on a wall where all employees can see them. Each job level is described and every employee gets to determine their own promotional trajectory and salary by voluntarily acquiring the skills from company mentors to prepare for the job they want.

Great leaders like Nick explanain the organization's approaches and standards to their people. They share the stories that give the company heart and soul and create a sense of belonging. They engender feelings of interest, pride, loyalty, commitment, grounding, engagement, confidence, and inspiration. A company's "why" connects employees to their organization's founder, to its early struggles and ultimate successes, to its hopes and dreams and goals, and to the other people who are a part of the history and story of that particular company.

An organization is healthy to the degree that it is consistent and complete; to the degree that management, operations, values and culture are all aligned. Healthy organizations are relatively free of politics and confusion. Their leaders are open to new ideas and the employees know exactly what to expect. Teams and team leaders care about one another and about the future of the organization so they come to the table with the right mindset and attitudes to sustain energy and engagement. In this "healthy home" environment employees never want to leave and they consistently outperform employees in typical organizations.

Nick was a construction worker before he opened Nick's Pizza and Pub. He had no direct experience running a restaurant and everyone told him he was crazy. He proved them all wrong. Not only has Nick defied conventional wisdom about what a fast food business can be and do, he cracked the motivational code and turned a bunch of high school kids into dream employees. He created a culture so successful that his little business has garnered national attention and acclaim, and his local community actively supports his business.

At the helm of highly effective and successful organizations we always a great leader with an open heart, a humble spirit and a healthy mindset. Nick used these to beat all the odds, and so can you.

"Those who turn good organizations into great organizations are motivated by a deep creative urge and an inner compulsion for sheer unadulterated excellence for its own sake."

James C. Collins

CHAPTER ELEVEN
Authentic Leadership

Leading an organization is much like leading a dance partner. To lead effectively so the dance is smooth and well executed, the leader must first learn and practice the dance steps and then learn the technique of leading another person. You can't learn that from a book. It's experiential. Once the steps and technique are mastered, a good lead dancer can make just about anyone look better on the dance floor.

As with dancing, leadership is mastered only by those who approach it with a passion for the art. Authentic leadership is not about business techniques, rules, processes and procedures so much as it is about the art of the dance. The techniques need to be known, of course, and rules, processes and procedures are necessary for creating healthy boundaries and structure, but great leaders have already mastered these and have turned their attention to creating conditions that nurture great performance and make people *want* to follow.

In his book *Primal Leadership*, Daniel Goleman observes, "Leaders drive emotions. When they drive them positively, they bring out everyone's best. When they drive emotions negatively, they spawn dissonance and undermine the emotional foundations that let people shine" (Goleman 2002). If we relate this to the dance, a great leader can make even a bad dancer look good, and a bad leader can make a great dancer look bad, and take all joy from the dance.

What Makes a Good Leader Great?

In his book *Good to Great,* Jim Collins described what he coined "Level 5 Leaders" His description was so far removed from the norm that we were inspired to conduct a study to discover what was beneath the unusual combination of traits Collins described. In our experience, leaders who are both willing to make hard decisions to get things done and humbly give credit to their people are about as rare as the Dodo bird and we wanted to know what drove these rare and highly effective behaviors. Because the CORE MAP assessment looks deeply and broadly enough to provide accurate measures of how well or poorly traits across the entire range of human behaviors are developed, and accurately predict competencies, coping strategies, reactionary patterns and emotional intelligence in specific areas, this is the tool we used to discover the underlying factors of leaders identified as Level 5.

Finding leaders who fit the criteria was no easy task. We queried hundreds of people and interviewed hundreds of leaders and found only a few. Those we chose for the study were validated as Level 5 Leaders by their employees, their peers and, sometimes, their vendors and customers. We asked that they take the CORE MAP assessment and then interviewed them to understand the trends we saw in the assessments. In interviewing these leaders, like Collins, we were struck by how genuinely humble and yet powerfully effective they were. On the surface, humility and power seem to be mutually exclusive. What we found is that in reality, they are both products of responsible authenticity. Genuine power is not the ability to make people do what you want them to do. It's the ability to inspire people to *want* to do what you want and feel good about it. Genuine power flows from a place of authenticity. Authentic people know who they are and what they want from life and there is no need to prove anything to anyone. They don't feel a need to protect some secret self they fear the world might see so they are free to connect at genuine levels. This openness results in their having unusual clarity and a longer view than most people which makes it easier to make wiser and more responsible choices for the good of all, which inspires others to do their best.

CORE is an acronym for Commander, Organizer, Relater and Entertainer; which describe a primary attribute of the four basic temperaments. Commanders are task oriented and driven to get things done. They are willing to step up to the plate and do whatever it takes to make things happen in an efficient way. Organizers are also task oriented, but they are driven to get things right. They prefer to focus on the task at hand to make sure it is done correctly. Relaters are people oriented and driven to get along with others. They humbly and naturally put the needs of others ahead of their own and are quick to give credit to others. Entertainers are also people oriented and driven to get connected. They want to be right in the middle of the arena experiencing everything first-hand.

The thing that struck us about the "tough and humble" pattern Collins described is the fact that these are traits of polar opposite types. Commander makes the tough decisions and Relater takes the humble position. These two styles are oppositions which have nothing in common. Commander is driven to succeed; Relater is laid-back and easy-going. Commander is bold and decisive; Relater is reserved and compliant. Commander is all about task completion; Relater is all about keeping people happy. In most people, to activate one style, the other gets suppressed. We wanted to see how that played out.

The "tough and humble" pattern presented on the CORE assessment as a well developed, but slightly impatient Commander (get it done) style, which was usually in the dominant or most preferred position, and a moderately-well developed and very patient Relater (get along) style, which was usually in the tertiary or backup position. Because the pattern suggesting slight impatience around getting things done and unusual patience in dealing with people appeared with such consistency, we began questioning study participants to understand it. One leader described the seemingly dichotomous pattern using a football analogy. "I surround myself with great players who I trust to do their job," he explained, "and when they are performing well, I am their biggest cheerleader. I am content to stand on the sidelines and revel in their performance. But, if they get to the one yard line and are fumbling the ball, I get out there and kick butt. They don't like it while it's happening, but when they make that touchdown, I'm the first guy they hug."

Another surprise was the close scores between thinking and feeling preferences. Most organizations value and promote the get-it-done Commander style and the get-it-right Organizer style, both of which are left-brain, thinking styles. The expression of feelings and emotions tend to be discouraged. Yet, in every case, the feeling function was full and rich in these exceptional leaders, which we labeled as VIP leaders because of three traits we invariably saw in these leaders. Each of them were Visionary, Influential and Progressive (VIP).

There is a palpable difference in organizations run by VIP leaders. When you walk into one, you know this is a genuinely people-centric organization. VIP leaders clearly believe their people are their most valuable asset and they actively look for ways to help them shine.

To download the free VIP Leader Study white paper, go to www.starperformancesystems.com or scan the QR Code.

It Pays to Be in Flow

Authenticity and disciplined strength are the foundation for the condition Claremont University professor and psychologist Mihaly Csikszentmihalyi describes as "flow" in his book of the same name. Csikszentmihalyi says, "The best moments in our lives are not the passive, receptive, relaxing times... The best moments usually occur when a person's body or mind is stretched to its limits in a voluntary effort to accomplish something challenging and worthwhile" (Csikszentmihalyi 2008, page 3)

Flow occurs when we are fully engaged and great leaders know how to create conditions for flow. The key aspect to flow, according to Csikszentmihalyi, is a sense of self-control and self-management. "In the flow-like state," he says, "we exercise control over the contents of our consciousness rather than allowing ourselves to be passively determined by external forces."

Though flow is an internal state, it can be inspired by a great leader. To inspire flow, leaders must first know their people well enough to know what will generate true interest and passion in those they seek to lead. Most leaders don't take the time to know their people that deeply. VIP leaders do because they understand how much more effective, engaged and dedicated their people will be, and how much easier that makes their job in the long run.

Jeff Gordon, the race car driver, Bruce Willis, the actor, and Terry Bradshaw, the sports commentator, excel at very different things, but they all have the same thing in common. All three men are doing what they fully believe they were born to do. Terry Bradshaw once said, "For a man who thought his best talent was throwing an inflated ellipsoid a long way, I've been fortunate in my career. In the end, I just discovered my real talent - being myself." Ultimately, that is everyone's real talent and great leaders have a knack for helping their people develop it to its highest potential.

Everyone is most effective when functioning in alignment with their authentic self, yet nearly eighty percent of the U.S. population is not doing that; a fact reflected in a number of studies. For example, a 2012 *Gallup* poll found that just 23% of employees felt their strengths were being utilized every day. 73% felt miscast in their role and said they never had the chance to reveal the best of themselves. A *Herman Trend Alert* study indicated that 50-80% of workers are in jobs for which their personality and interests are not well matched. Our research suggests that 54% of the U.S. adult population have no idea who they are authentically or what they are passionate about and 97% are not living up to their full potential.

Three Attributes of Great Leaders (VIPs)

- **Authentic Self-Awareness & Expression**

  Great leaders know who they are and are comfortable expressing themselves authentically. This includes expressing their feeling side, which is well-developed in VIP leaders. In ordinary leaders the feeling function is suppressed because most corporations discourage it.

  Authentic self-awareness is something every team member needs. When a person knows who they are and has the freedom to perform in a way that is congruent with their authentic self, they are happier and far more productive. Well placed, self-aware employees are as much as 400% more effective than those who are not, both in their work and in the way they interact with others. When people operate against their true nature, they are ineffective, unhappy, disengaged, problematical, and costing organizations a lot of time and money.

- **Accurate Awareness of Others**

  Great leaders take the time to know their people - really know them. They don't just know who their people are, they know what they want. They know their strengths and their limitations. They know what keeps them fired up and what drains them of energy and interest. And because they know and care, they also know how to get the best from their people.

Daniel Akerson, Chairman and Chief Executive Officer of General Motors, observed "There are certain values our leaders must instill in our organization: that customers are our compass; relationships matter; and, individual excellence is crucial. As leaders, we must emulate these values in all that we do and drive accountability throughout the organization – a firm sense that results and integrity count. If we operate with these values in mind, we can achieve our vision" (Akerson 2013).

This is good advice, but to follow it requires more than most leaders have available to them. Individual excellence is a product of engaged, intrinsically-driven people. To have self-driven people who perform with excellence requires a much different approach than most management practices take. To influence others to perform at their best, leaders need to know what their people need, and how to help them get it.

Until you have fully engaged employees, customers cannot serves as a compass because those who interact with customers most closely are not engaged and dedicated to doing excellent work on the customer's behalf. Disengaged employees don't even bother to try to serve customers well, much less take the time to discover what customers really want and need, what they are concerned about, what keeps them loyal or what drives them away.

Relationships do matter and, individual excellence is certainly a crucial component for success, but before organizations can have excellent relationships with their customers, they have to have meaningful relationships with their employees. Before they can get to individual excellence, they have to have engaged teams that support one another.

- **Effective Self-Management**

  Self-management begins with emotional intelligence; understanding and managing our own emotions as well as considering, and being considerate of, the emotions of others. To be effective at self-management, we have to be comfortable enough with our own feelings to express them openly, authentically and in beneficial ways.

Feelings, not facts, drive performance. All true motivation is intrinsically driven and all intrinsic motivation is based in feelings.

Like assertiveness, the ability to motivate intrinsically is a learned skill and is a vitally important one for leaders. Our *Applied Intrinsic Motivation* (AIM) program was developed as a result of working with leaders, managers, salespeople and other key personnel, and discovering that most of them had the desire, but lacked ability, to identify intrinsic motivators and foster them in others.

To successfully transition from the expensive and time consuming extrinsic motivation model to the highly effective intrinsic model, is largely a matter of awareness on a deeper level than most developmental programs provide. To our delight, we have found that most leaders learn the intrinsic motivation model with relative ease and quickly incorporate it into their leadership style once they know what to look for and how to apply it.

EQ and IQ

Most leaders today are aware of the difference between emotional intelligence, sometimes referred to as EQ or EI, and IQ, or mental intelligence. Leading researchers have concluded that EQ is a much better predictor of success than IQ, both on and off the job. We have all seen highly educated people who lead train wreck lives. The "educated derelict" President Calvin Coolidge referred to in his famous quote "Press On" is not all that uncommon, many leaders and managers have horror stories about highly credentialed employees who wreaked havoc in their organization.

EQ develops around the two primary factors: self-awareness and self-management. Self-awareness leads to greater self-confidence, guides values and belief systems, and builds healthy levels of self-esteem. Self-management is the means by which we master our emotions, manage impulses and gain level of self-control that inspire confidence in others.

A study conducted by Pearson and Porath of thousands of managers and employees concluded that behaviors associated with low EQ, such as angry outbursts, rude comments, incivility, and moodiness led to stress, burnout and anxiety in the workplace and resulted in:

- Two-thirds of employees reporting that their performance declined
- Four out of five employees reported that they had lost significant work time worrying about an unpleasant incident
- 63% wasted time avoiding the low EQ offender
- More than 75% of respondents said that their commitment to their low EQ employer had waned. This was true whether the low EQ behaviors were observed in a manager and were tolerated in employees
- 37% resigned due to the low EQ behavior in a boss
- 12% resigned due to the low EQ behavior in a co-worker

High EQ Leads to:

- Better collaboration
- Greater productivity
- Higher morale
- Increased employee tenure
- Increased job satisfaction
- Effective use of humor as a strategy
- Increased job and company engagement
- Better communication inside and outside of teams
- A greatly improved bottom line
  (Bell 2014)

Twelve Steps to Authentic Leadership

1. Invite and embrace learning. No matter how much expertise a leader brings to the role, there is always room to grow. The number one role of leadership is motivating people to greatness, which requires an extensive knowledge of human nature. Stay open to learning through formal training and coaching, and from others, including your team members and front line workers.

2. Be patient with yourself. Most high level leaders lead with the Commander trait-set and are hard-wired to be impatient. Commander's primary need is to get things done and impatience is what drives that. Feeling impatient is not the issue; it's how you handle it. Allow impatience to drive performance, but don't let it derail you.

3. Communicate clearly. Keep your team fully informed, not just of projects, goals, priorities and deadlines, but of *why* they are important and how they make a difference. Also, get and give regular feedback to ensure that your people clearly understand what you expect.

4. Ask great questions and *listen*. Good questions let you know what's important to your people. Listening to the answers lets your team know that you want to know about their legitimate concerns. Good questions challenge our thinking. They reframe and redefine the problem and remind us of what is important. Great leaders use the power of questions to understand themselves, help others increase awareness and keep their team focused on the goal.

5. Set a good example. Demand the same level of professionalism from yourself that you expect and hope to foster in others. Leaders who fail to walk their talk are not trusted or respected.

6. Recognize performance and honest effort. Build the confidence and commitment of your team members by openly recognizing their efforts as well as their achievements.

7. Discourage complaining or gripe sessions. Let your people know you are happy to participate in finding solutions, but will not tolerate whining or complaining.

8. Give your team a top-of-the-mountain view. Explain to your team how the projects they are working on fit into the company's larger goals and how those larger goals benefit the people and community your company serves.

An example of this is Anne Mulcahy, the chairman and CEO of Xerox, who was largely responsible for orchestrating what *Money Magazine* called "the great turnaround story of the post-crash era." By keeping the company steadfastly focused on employees and customers, she was able to lead Xerox away from the brink of collapse to become one of the world's most profitable and innovative technology and service enterprises.

"Even while Rome was burning," Mulcahy said, "people wanted to know what the city of the future would look like." This, she explained, was also true of the Xerox organization. When the end seemed to be approaching, the question employees and investors wanted her to answer most was "what will Xerox look like after it comes through this period of survival and turnaround."

To help create clarity, and focus her people on a new shared vision of the future, Mulcahy and her team wrote a fictional *Wall Street Journal* article, dated 2005, that detailed exactly what the company looked like. "We outlined the things we hoped to accomplish as though we had already achieved them," said Mulcahy. "We included performance metrics—even quotes from Wall Street analysts. It was really our vision of what we wanted the company to become. Xerox has gone a long way to making its vision a reality. Looking back on the article now, I'd say we've already accomplished about 80 percent of things we set out to do," she said (Gregersen 2014).

Considering Xerox's great turnaround, it's clear the top-of-the-mountain view Mulcahy helped her people gain provided an effective blueprint the team could buy into and work toward.

9. Guide like a Sherpa. Sherpas are professional guides who help people get to the top of a mountain. They provide the tools and the expertise, and help climbers get past difficult spots, but allow them to climb on their own to the best of their capacity. By providing the tools and resources climbers need, they provide a structured freedom environment and a team mindset that allows each climber, from novice to pro, to perform to their highest potential and ascend the mountain together. Adopt the Sherpa model to take your people to the top.

10. Create an environment of constant learning and development, and include yourself. Learning occurs on many levels. People learn from mistakes in the right environment and they learn from gaining new information and skills. Allow mistakes, provided learning occurs and the mistake is corrected. Provide developmental training appropriate to individual needs. Remember: the emerging workforce expects it, especially Millennials, who tend to stay in a workplace only as long as they feel like they are learning and growing.

11. Stay ahead of the curve. Bureaucracies, such as the U.S. government, are famous for being behind the curve of innovation and change. Be sure you are not in that boat. It can cost you a lot of time and money, and a lot of lost talent.

An example is a system developed in the United States by Dr. W. Edwards Deming, an American statistician, professor, author, lecturer, and consultant, which he first presented to the U.S. government. They rejected it so Deming offered the system to Japan. They immediately saw its usefulness and from 1950 onward, Deming taught top business managers in Japan how to improve product design and quality using the method known today as Kaizen.

The basic concept of Kaizen is to innovate to meet requirements and increase productivity. Kaizen is about taking small, incremental steps towards ultimate perfection as opposed to taking big steps that can require huge investments and result in great loss if the innovation falls short.

Over time, Kaizen became a revolution around the world and twenty-five years after the U.S. government rejected the system and Japan adopted it, U.S. corporations were investing millions of dollars sending consultants to Japan to learn the system their government had rejected. In the interim, Japanese auto and technology manufacturers pulled ahead of U.S. manufacturers and claimed a big chunk of the market in those arenas. Though we may be able to calculate the cost in years, the cost in dollars to U.S. manufacturers is incalculable.

Something similar is happening today in the way employees are being managed and developed. Employers in other countries realized several years ago that the coaching and apprenticeship models worked far better with the newer generations and in the current fast-paced marketplace, so they revived the model and began adjusting their leadership styles. Unfortunately, most U.S. leaders have not followed suit.

According to Wall Street Journal contributor, Peter Downs, the number of apprenticeship programs in the U.S. has fallen by one-third in the last decade. With only 330,578 registered apprentices in 2013, the U.S. reported less than 40% of the number reported in Britain, a country one-fifth as populous. U.S. leaders have also been very slow to adopt the more collaborative coaching approach to leadership.

There are glimmers of hope though as a few savvy leaders have begun applying the coaching and apprenticeship models and reporting stellar results. Sampatkumar B. Aratti, VP at Lapp India says, "Leadership is an apprentice trade. With the evolving needs of business and a rapidly changing scenario in the modern workplace, the demands and dynamics of leadership have acquired new meaning. To be a good leader in the present ecosystem is not easy, it requires an ability to adjust to uncertain circumstances, competing demands and evolving challenges" (Aratti 2013).

People do not learn leadership from books. They can get a lot of good pointers from books, but new leaders learn best from more experienced leaders. Leadership is learned about 20% in the classroom and from books and 80% on the job so leaders who want to foster great leadership need to know how to coach and mentor. The apprenticeship approach is completely different than most leaders are accustomed to and most need mentoring themselves to make the transition to this more effective style. Our Choice Leadership program follows the appreticeship learning model (20% training and 80% experiential application) and we have found this approach yields far better results. The apprenticeship model provides an opportunity to master a craft, including leadership, on the job while dealing with different situations and learning from a mentor how to fit into an effective leadership role.

12. Be an Influencer. Influential leaders are masters at balancing decisiveness and consideration. They develop decisiveness because they know people find it difficult to follow leaders who continually change their minds. Influential leaders don't throw out unexamined decisions. They do a thorough SWOT analysis to identify strengths, weaknesses, opportunities and threats, then they make a decision and stick with it.

On the consideration side, influencers inspire through creating a greater sense of connectivity and friendliness in a structured freedom environment, and through knowing how to tap into intrinsic motivators. They understand the importance of meaningful work. They encourage innovation, creativity and independent work, and regularly take steps to ensure their people develop to their highest potential.

A Deeper Perspective

In the book, *Outliers*, author Malcolm Gladwell suggests that it takes 10,000 hours of focused and dedicated practice within a specific niche to become an expert (*Gladwell 2008*).

This idea was reinforced by a long-term study conducted by psychologist K. Anders Ericsson where he compared three groups of violinists at the Academy of Music in Berlin. The first group consisted of star pupils, the second good students and the third students who would probably never play professionally. The groups started training at the age of five and in the beginning they all practiced roughly the same amount of time. Around eight years of age the difference in commitment to the craft started to become obvious. Ericsson recorded the numbers of hours practiced each week and found that by the age of twenty, amateur musicians had logged a total of 2,000 hours of practice while the elite violinists had practiced 10,000 hours or more (Ericsson, Krampe, and Clemens 1993).

Such studies challenge the premise that genius or giftedness is purely a matter of innate talent. They suggest that innate talent plays a lesser role in achieving expert status than one might think. Gladwell came to the conclusion that the correlation between good and expert was clearly delineated by the amount of practice the musicians put in. What he failed to consider was *why* the dedicated musicians were committed enough to put in all those hours. It's true that quality practice makes perfect, but what drives quality practice is *passion*, and passion is a product of innate talent on the right path.

The field Ericcson and Gladwell studied, music, is generally pursued for its own sake. Rarely are people encouraged to pursue artistic avenues as a way to make a living so, without an innate passion for music, few people would work at perfecting it. Still, there are those who have the passion, but fail to practice enough to become great. This disparity generally exists because the less dedicated student has less innate passion for that particular art form, or because parental pressures or the instructor's teaching style has diminished it.

Unlike the arts, people are frequently encouraged to take a leadership role. There are clear benefits to being a leader; more money, more clout, more power, greater flexibility, and better perks just to name a few. In large organizations, passion for leading people is rarely considered. Many managers and leaders have been put into that role by default. Many more aspire to the role, not because they love the practice of leading, but because they want the power, position and clout. These reasons don't typically translate into great performance as a leader. Getting people to want to follow and perform well is an art as well as a set of skills. Both require practice.

The belief that the number of hours dedicated to a pursuit results in high performance is widespread and is primarily the reason most companies default to more training whenever an employee is not performing up to par rather than taking the time to understand the issue and get to the core of the matter. It's easy to send people off for training believing someone can "fix them." It's easy to imagine that with enough hours of exposure to skills training, an ineffective employee will perform at higher levels. But that rarely occurs when the passion that drives performance is lacking. Add lack of passion to low natural capacity for that particular skill and any effort made to improve performance is a waste of time and money.

Research conducted by the Association for Talent Development (ATD - formerly ASTD) estimated that about one-third of organizational training focuses on managerial and supervisory skills, mandatory and compliance training, and profession- or industry-specific training. The remaining two-thirds covers topics such as processes and procedures, customer service, sales training, and executive development (Miller 2014).

Another study suggests that much of the 52 plus billion dollars organizations spend on training each year is essentially lost money. This is supported by a study reported on in *Chief Learning Officer Magazine* which stated that the overall effectiveness of typical training is on average only about 20%. The study concluded that typical training produced only minor changes in 60% of attendees and was ineffective for 20%, meaning there was no discernible change (Cross 2006).

On the surface, this seems to be a case for *not* training employees at all. In reality it is a strong case for not training employees in a *general manner* without knowing what they are interested in learning. It's a case for first making sure employees want the training being offered and see value in learning the material. Before any kind of training can be effective, the trainee has to be *interested* in learning. Otherwise, they just dutifully show up and keep a seat occupied.

Continual learning is a good practice, provided the students are engaged. In any development program, interest in learning should be the first consideration.

CHAPTER TWELVE
A System for Success

Most leaders and organizational consultants hold to the idea that business is about three things; *product, process,* and *people.* Most attend to business in that order, with product as the basis for business, process the secondary consideration, and finally the people who will make the products and manage the processes.

We contend that there are *four* primary elements to business and that to be highly successful, the order needs to shift. The fourth element is *purpose* and, based on today's most successful business models, it should be the foundation upon which the other three factors rest. The order for organizations that want to thrive into the future should be purpose, people, product and process. We focus wholly on purpose and people because they are so vital to success, and their importance is so frequently overlooked. Purpose has always been important, but the importance is compounded for Millennials. Failure to convey the organization's purpose, and for that purpose to be real and meaningful, is a deal breaker for them.

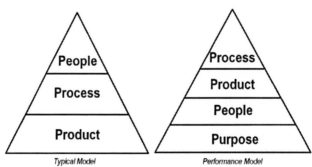

Typical Model   Performance Model

Illustration 12.1

The big question in many organizations when it comes to people is how to find and keep high performers. While this appears to be people focused, it's usually about getting the product out. Having people who can keep systems humming and products flowing are certainly important, but when that is the main focus, the fuel that runs the vehicle is being drained off.

For organizations to remain viable into the future, the focus needs to be on creating a culture and environment which not only attracts and retains high performers, but also supports and sustains them. If the culture and environment don't support high performance employees, attracting them is a waste of effort because they are not likely to stay and those that do stay won't be fully engaged. It's like gathering seeds without bothering to prepare the ground to receive them. You can buy the best seeds there are, but if they are planted in poor, unprepared soil they will not germinate and grow. The same is true of "planting" people into an organization. If the culture is healthy and the ground prepared, even less than hardy employees can grow and thrive, and top performers soar.

The core purpose of an organization is like True North on a compass. Without it, people have nothing to align themselves with and without alignment they are not motivated to do their jobs well. In organizations where the culture provides fertile ground, people have a clear sense of direction. There is cohesion, cooperation and the sense of belonging that inspires high levels of motivation and performance.

To provide fertile ground, leaders need to do a lot more than give pep talks, hand out awards and "incentives," call group meetings, and throw company parties. These can be nice additions, but if they don't align with employee needs, they are just exercises in futility and can actually be detrimental.

A client of ours, a Fortune 500 company, had been functioning under a command and control leader for several years and employees who had been with the company for awhile were those who were aligned with that leadership style. When the parent company spun off a major division, the leader chosen for that division had a very different style. This leader understood the value of teamwork and employee cohesion and, in an effort to change the culture to a more employee-friendly one, he began requiring participation at company sponsored social functions. These were meant to provide an informal setting where employees on all level could meet and connect. The leader expected great joy and full participation to follow. He got that from only about 15% the workforce.

The majority railed against the changes. The new, upbeat and very well intentioned leader was baffled.

We found that the old command and control culture had attracted a lot of left-brain, serious, lone eagle types and they considered the required social gatherings to be a frivolous waste of time. The solution was as simple as enlightening the leader and suggesting that he make the gatherings an *option,* rather than a requirement, and present it as an opportunity for growth and development. This simple shift completely changed the dynamic and before long most employees had opted to attend the gatherings. Those who didn't were free to hole up in their offices or cubicles during social events as long as they actively participated in team meetings. Though the leader's intentions were good, being required to participate left most of the employees feeling disempowered and resentful. Once they were given a choice and could see the benefits, most were happy to align with the leader's vision.

Like the well-intentioned leader above, many leaders create problems without intending to. Understanding employees on a deeper level and meeting them where they live can eliminate much of that.

To break through the outdated and largely ineffective assumptive leadership model and create a high performance environment, begin thinking about and planning toward are the answers to the following questions:

- What changes need to occur to be sure we are building a healthy Structured Freedom culture?
- What will best support individual results as well as team contributions? (Hint: Ask your people and listen to their answers.)
- How wide is the gap between a healthy culture that will work for every generation of employees and the one we now have?
- How do we best bridge that gap?
- What will best practices look like in this new environment?
- What will best practices need to look like when Millennials make up the majority of our workforce?
- What changes do I need to make personally to be a Level 5 VIP leader?

In a structured freedom environment, best practices are more about creating transparency and trust in a collaborative environment than about creating new systems or processes. Focus on intrinsic motivators and you will greatly increase your odds of getting the very best from each of your employees, no matter what generation they identify with.

Implementing the changes necessary to prepare for the inevitable power shift isn't as hard, and won't take nearly as long, as many employers fear if they are focused on the right things. Intrinsically motivated people can accomplish amazing things in record time.

The fact that Millennials respect the knowledge of superiors and actively seek collaborative relationships provides huge opportunities to the right kinds of leaders. Those who know how to tap into the great potential this generation will ride the new wave to successes beyond what many even imagine. Google, Facebook, Zappos, and other Millennial-friendly organizations that have gone from a mere idea to multi-billion dollar organizations in just a few years provide a preview of what is possible for those who know how to influence Generation X and Millennials.

Both generations came into an uncertain, topsy-turvy world. The difference is Gen X looked at what they inherited and decided the wise thing was to live for the moment. Give them a healthy environment in whihc to work and they are generally happy. That is not the case for Millennials. Though they grew up is the same uncertain world as Gen X, they took a whold different approach. Millennials decided they had to do something to change the world they inherited, and the change had to make a real difference. Meaningful work is a core value for Millennials; one that isn't going to change. Leaders who can provide them with meaningful work and convey how it is making a significant difference in the world will gain their undying loyalty and can get the same high performance and outcomes companies like Google have gotten. Those who don't can kiss high performance employees goodbye and resign themselves to mediocrity.

What can you expect from Millennials? An example is Craig Kielburger who as a 12-year-old full of hope and vigor, set out to change the world. Though Kielburger knew there were things that couldn't be changed, that awareness didn't dampen his spirit or his commitment to make a difference in places where he could. He founded a charity for children called *Free the Children*, which has now been in operation for 17 years. Today, the charity he founded in his parent's living room has made a difference for over a million children and families living in desperate poverty in 45 countries around the world. The organization takes in $30 million a year and is the largest organization of children helping children in the world.

It all began in the 1990s when Kielburger read about a boy in Pakistan who was killed for trying to stop child labor. Rather than just see the injustice of it, he decided to do something. He talked his parents into taking him to Asia and, with the help of activists and government officials, helped shut down sweatshops and brothels manned by children. His determination to expose child poverty has helped him recruit two million volunteers, and almost all of whom were under the age of 18 when they volunteered.

According to a 60 Minutes broadcast (11/21/12), *Free the Children* builds schools, provides clean water, and helps artisans sell their goods in an effort to help people rise out of poverty. As Kielburger and many like him have demonstrated, a true and very positive power shift can happen when a Millennial is inspired to make a difference.

To tap into the Millennial mindset and benefit from it requires that leaders adopt a new mindset in four areas:

1. Leadership practices

2. Environment/Culture

3. Employee/Employer Relationships

4. The Vehicle

Leadership Practices

We have presented examples of effective leadership throughout this book to make the point that a VIP Leader is a very different kind of leader on every level. As a supervisor, a VIP leader takes on the role of coach or mentor and uses an apprenticeship model to teach employees the skills they need to succeed. As the employee becomes more and more proficient, the VIP supervisor shifts to coaching as needed. The collaborative relationship Millennials crave is always there.

C-level leaders don't spend as much face time with front-line employees, of course, but they are still accessible and collaborative in their approach. VIP leaders take a supportive, rather than directive approach. They make sure mid-level managers are supported and have the tools and awareness they need to provide the level and kind of support their employees need to succeed. They make it a point to connect with their people on every level, not as a ruler, but as an integral part of the team.

To Be a VIP Leader:

1. **Be a Visionary.** Visionary leaders begin with the vision and use processes to support it. They make sure goals and the steps for reaching them are very clear to all team members, especially those who will be performing the tasks. Thay make sur ethey have the right people in the right seats and that they are proficient at the job they are doing. They provide the vison and the framework and then give the employee the freedom to bring the vision to life.

   In his book, *Maestro: A Surprising Story About Leading by Listening,* Roger Nierenberg talks about the powerful leadership lessons that can be learned from the subtleties of observing a world class orchestra. "The most important thing a conductor brings to the orchestra is a vision of the music that the musicians will want to bring to life with their playing. If a leader wants his people to truly own the work then he has to be willing to let go of some control."

   Nierenberg adds, "When I step onto the podium, my every action should provide answers to questions such as where are we going? What's the goal? What are our priorities? How do we create a compelling and powerful performance of this piece? What's our plan for getting there? And, very important, exactly what do the musicians need to do to contribute? You see, a strong vision can lead people away from focusing on their part alone and toward being aware of the whole. The vision should be lofty enough to stir and challenge people. If it's too limited, then people will feel underutilized and uninspired. But when the musicians take hold of a vision then they attach their playing to it. Tasks that might have previously seemed routine now acquire meaning and beauty. While they are doing their jobs, they're always thinking of the grand vision."

"Eventually," he continues, "I realized that a great performance would happen only when the motivation sprang as much from them as from me. I learned to see my job as simply creating an environment where that could happen. Once I learned to engage their artistry, everything felt so much easier" (Ericsson, Prietula and Cokely 2007).

The Visionary Path to High Performance

- Define the grand vision
- Get the right people on your team
- Convey the vision to your people and get buy in
- Determine the process
- Work with your team to lay out the roadmap
- Define milestones and touch points
- Teach the specific steps for superb performance
- Keep polishing to ensure proficiency
- Turn the process over to the performers and invite them to "plus it"
- Continue to hold the dream and the vision in front of them
- Refine as necessary to reach excellence

2. **Be Influential.** There are only four ways to get people to act:

   1. Guilt
   2. Fear
   3. Force
   4. Influence

Of the four, only influence is healthy and beneficial. Unfortunately, it is also the method least used. The order in which the inducements are presented above is how they are typically applied. Most people never get to the fourth option because they have created a negative situation before then and the opportunity to positively influence is lost.

Typically, people try to get what they want through guilt first. If that doesn't work, they move to fear (threats of consequences). If that doesn't work, they move to force (do it or else). The usual response is resistance and counter-aggression, often in the form of doing as little as possible for the individual applying the first three tactics. Influential leaders bypass the first three and go straight to the fourth.

The reason most people don't use influence is because it takes more effort initially. In the long run, however, it is by far the most efficient and effective way to get things done. To influence, you must:

- Know your people
- Show an interest in them as individuals, not just as workers
- Engage them in meaningful conversations (use appreciative inquiry to ask high value questions and listen with genuine interest)
- Build trust (occurs over time through positive experiences)

Appreciative inquiry, which for many requires a change in mindset and a shift away from the typical problem-centered approach, helps people discover and focus on what works so they can do more of it. Through this form of inquiry, untold stories begin to develop; patterns emerge, individuals tap into positive achievements and begin narrations that strengthen and inspire. Appreciative inquiry doesn't ignore problems—it just approaches them from the perspective of what *is* working rather than what is *not* working.

In General, Appreciative Inquiry:

- Is thought-provoking
- Expands possibilities
- Focuses attention
- Brings underlying assumptions to light
- Stimulates curiosity and creativity
- Stimulates reflective thinking and more creative responses
- Can help a group move forward faster and in a more positive direction

As you move from simple yes/no questions to "what if we could" or "how can we," people become engaged in the process and begin to contribute ideas few would have initially imagined. Walt Disney was a master of Appreciative Inquiry. His trademark question, "How can we plus it?" which generally followed an excited exclamation of "This is great!" is an example of Appreciative Inquiry. It is a very effective way to discover and manage beliefs and values, and build trust.

To be influential, we must start where a person lives. We must know what's important to them; what fires them up. Appreciative Inquiry can take you a long way toward that end.

3. **Be Progressive.** Progressive leaders are forward thinking. They don't cling to past standards because they worked in the past. They realize that as the world, marketplaces and people change, and so must the structure of the organization. They are always looking for ways to "plus it" as Disney did. They understand that the organization is only as good as its people and they are fanatical about making sure they have the right people and that their people are well trained and supported. They are never satisfied with good. Their vision and goal is greatness, and they realize they can only achieve that by keeping really good people who are enthusiastic about the company and their job.

In his book, *How to Win Friends and Influence People*, Dale Carnegie quoted pioneer business man, Charles Schwab, who said, "I consider my ability to arouse enthusiasm among my people the greatest asset I possess, and the way to develop the best in a person is by appreciation and encouragement. There is nothing else that so kills the ambitions of a person as criticisms from superiors" (**Carnegie 1936**). Great leaders have always been ahead of their time and way ahead of the pack. Carnegie's book is filled with sage advice yet nearly eighty years later few leaders have adopted it.

Progressive leaders have always understood the benefit of knowing their people and of focusing on what they are doing *right* rather than on what they are doing wrong. As Schwab observed, there is only one way to get people to do anything and that's to make them *want* to do it. People want to feel good about themselves and focusing on what they are doing right is a great way to do that. And there's a secondary benefit many don't realize they are getting. Recent brain research suggests that what we focus on expands the capacity of the brain to produce it. So by pointing out what an employee is doing right, leaders not only encourage more of that behavior, they actually help their employee increase the capacity to perform the task.

ENVIRONMENT/CULTURE

As has been presented throughout this book, a healthy culture is one of structured freedom where people know exactly what is expected of them, exactly what will happen when they perform well, and exactly what will happen when they don't. And where they have a lot of freedom to perform in their own way within those very clear and consistently enforced boundaries.

Most companies are quite comfortable with creating boundaries, but not so comfortable allowing employees freedom to perform in their own way. This is where the mindset of many leaders needs to shift. Employees who require a lot of freedom (which includes most Gen Xers and Millennials, and *all* people whose work is based on innovation and creative thought) resent being restricted. Resentment creates stress, and stress reduces the capacity to perform well. Many leaders know this, but are still reluctant to build the structure and environment that would afford employees the freedom to perform at optimal levels.

Jeff Weiner, CEO of LinkedIn, is a classic example of a leader who is working to produce and sustain a healthy environment. Reportedly, he ends his meetings and speeches by asking what he could have done better. He works right alongside his employees and his workdays are just as long as theirs, and he takes the time to acknowledge even their small accomplishments. In meetings, when it's clear someone has made a mistake, Weiner displays a deft touch, turning the gaffe into a teaching moment for everyone. Weiner's style earns raves from his staff. His Mountain View, California-based company with more than 3,000 employees and 350 million members consistently ranks as one of the best places to work. LinkedIn had a 92 percent employee-approval rating in an anonymous survey performed by Glassdoor in 2013. Weiner creates clear boundaries, but he also gives his people a lot of latitude and is lavish with his time and attention.

As a leader, you are going to spend time on something. You will be busy either cracking the whip and keeping problems at bay or inspiring your people to greatness. Those who are good at the latter have found the role of leader to be a lot more fun and effective, and a lot more profitable too.

EMPLOYER/EMPLOYEE RELATIONSHIPS

The next area of importance is the employer/employee relationship. The currently held view of leadership is that leaders need to remain above and apart from employees to maintain the established hierarchy. That doesn't fly with Millennials. They want collaborative leaders and are quick to reject hierarchies. To keep performers in the future, leaders will need to change the way they view the employer/employee relationship. They will need to become less like the typical CEO and more like the orchestra conductor. They will need to be visible and accessible to engage their people and keep them interested and fully engaged. They will need to learn how to tap into the genius of key employees and become a catalyst for developing them to their highest potential so they can do the same for their teams.

The most effective way to get the best from your people and build a healthy, collaborative relationship is through a coaching/mentoring model that uses appreciative inquiry and intrinsic motivation methods. Throughout recorded history this has been the way people have learned and developed best. Kings and dictators may rule territories, but they never win the minds or loyalties of the people. Positive influencers do. The world of business today is one of knowledge and technology. Both require that minds be fully engaged, and the only way to keep them engaged is to keep people happy and intrinsically motivated. That's possible only when leaders know what their people really want and need, and how to help them get it.

A FUNCTIONAL "VEHICLE"

Your business is your vehicle. It gets you from where you are to where you want to go in the world of enterprise. Obviously, you need the vehicle before you start gathering people, but it is *people* that drive the vehicle and keep it functional. The trust people have in one another, or the lack thereof, determines how quickly or slowly the vehicle moves forward and how effectively it navigates changing conditions. No matter how great the idea or the purpose of the business, without a trustworthy leader and dedicated, high performance people, the vehicle will eventually come to a stop.

A Trustworthy Leader

Employees want to know whether their boss or employer cares about and is committed to them, especially through significant change events. Trust is a key component of all aspects of leadership especially in times of stress. As people go through a change, there is a corresponding loss of direction and of confidence unless there is a trustworthy leader at the helm demonstrating care and commitment and keeping people informed.

In *Managing the Dynamics of Change*, Jerald Jellison uses a J-curve to demonstrate the process of change. This applies to all kinds of change; personal, organizational and technological.

Based on the J-curve model (*illustration 12.2*), people are most vulnerable at the point at which they first confront change, and things tend to get worse before they get better. That is exactly when care, trust, commitment and clear communication are most needed. Pushing for performance will not get an organization past the initial drop in energy, focus and performance faster. In fact it does just the opposite. Realize that change is not immediate or linear. There is a learning curve and initially things seem more difficult. It's at these times your people need inspiration most.

In *The Speed of Trust,* Stephen M. R. Covey states that trust is "the one thing that changes everything" and that "the number one job of any leader is to inspire trust... to release the creativity and capacity of individuals to give their best..." *(Covey, 2006)*

Based on extensive research, Covey found that trust always affects two outcomes; speed and cost. "When trust is low," he observes, "speed goes down and cost goes up. When trust is high, speed goes up and cost goes down." In other words, trust moves people through change faster and generally shortens the learning curve as people become more willing to risk something new. But there can be no trust without transparency. To the degree that leaders withhold information from their people, trust will be lacking. That includes information about their job, your expectations, what other departments are doing and why, how the employee fits into the overall picture, what the company is doing and why, and about you, their leader.

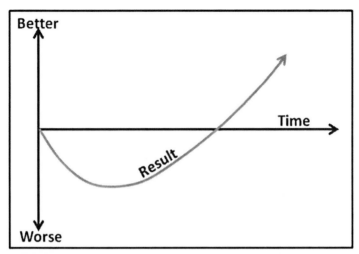

During Change Events, People Do Worse Before They Do Better

Illustration 12.2

To Build Trust:

1. Make and keep commitments to yourself and those you lead.

2. Function from a place of integrity and good character. Be honest. Let people know where you stand. Tell it like it is rather than distorting facts.

3. Focus on results, not activities, and generously give credit to others where credit is due.

4. Communicate your expectations clearly. Let people know where the change is headed and how it will impact the company and employees. Share both the good and the bad so employees know what to expect and can prepare.

5. Communicate what you need from your people, what you expect, what the rewards are for exemplary performance, and what the consequences are for poor performance.

6. Be very consistent and fair in your actions. Do what you say you will do and be sure company policies and practices apply to all people on every level all the time.

7. Stay humble and avoid making assumptions. Be a continual learner and be willing to learn from everyone no matter what their position or title. Most organizations are full of untapped brilliance. Consciously look for it in your organization.

High Performance People

Many leaders believe they have to choose between structure and freedom. They don't see how two seemingly opposing conditions can co-exist, but the two are, in fact, perfect and essential complements. The best organizational environments are built around a healthy dose of both. *Illustration 12.3* shows the effects of an imbalance in either direction and of organizations where both structure and freedom are in balance.

A great example of high structure and high freedom is a race car pit crew. According to Breon Klopp, senior director of development at PIT, an industry leader in pit crew training, top-ranked NASCAR pit crews reduced pit stop times from an average of 29 seconds in 1989 to 13 seconds in 2014. That's a 223% improvement in efficiency.

No doubt better equipment has something to do with this, but equipment is only as good as the people using it. Race teams have achieved such impressive results by hiring people who are more physically, mentally and emotionally fit, and giving them the best tools and the training they need. They establish specific job descriptions, set clear expectations, carefully analyze the results and keep fine-tuning. That's the structure part of the equation.

There has also been a culture change that places more value on teamwork, acknowledges the contributions of the pit crew, and shows more appreciation for a job well done. Klopp maintains businesses can implement similar changes and see similar positive results. "Too many companies have the wrong people in the wrong jobs," he asserts, "or their jobs aren't clearly defined, or they don't have adequate training or the right tools to do their jobs. These are the specifics companies can focus on, using the pit crew model" (Jacobus 2009).

What organization wouldn't want to have their vehicle operating as efficiently as a winning race car and their team functioning as effectively as a pit crew? The trick is how you get there, which brings us back to the capacity, skills and interest formula we presented in chapter six.

Capacity is the *natural ability* to do the job. Interest is the *desire* to do the job. Skills are learned and come from practice. Practice best adds to our capacity quotient when it complements our natural capabilities.

Practicing to become a fast runner, for example, will increase the ability to run faster only to the extent of the individual's capabilities. An individual with a stocky build and bulky muscles who is built for strength will never be abe to run as fast as a lean, agile individual naturally built for speed. Practice could certainly improve the ability to run faster, but only to a point. In this case, the desire is there, but the capacity is missing. Excellence requires both capacity and interest, combined with intrinsically driven motivation and correct application (the right kind of practice). Here's how the high performance formula lays out:

Capacity + Interest = Performance Potential

Performance Potential + Intrinsic Motivation = Commitment

Commitment + Correct Practice = Star Performance

Corporate Environments

	High Structure Low	
High **Freedom** **Low**	**Structured Freedom** Clarity Motivation Low Mistakes High Trust High Satisfaction	**No Consequences** Confusion High Stress High Mistakes Low Trust Low Satisfaction
	No Mistakes Fear / High Stress No Innovation Low Mistakes Low Trust Low Satisfaction	**Firefighter** Frustration High Stress High Mistakes Low Trust Low Satisfaction

Illustration 12.3

Celebrating Success

"Okay. Great Job! What's next?" asks a leader in a workshop upon completing a challenge. "What about taking the time to celebrate your success?" we respond. "Hey! I'm here to learn. Let's move on," he urges. Get it done and move on is a typical response from leaders. They get so caught up in day-to-day activities that they neglect to celebrate their successes and those of their people and, though most are not aware of it, skipping this step is costing them plenty.

A common productivity-draining pattern we see on CORE assessments occurs as a result of giving too much energy to getting things done and devoting too little time to celebrating success and re-energizing the mind and body.

"What's next?" may seem like enthusiasm, but when accomplishment is not balanced with reward, "what's next" diminishes our capacity to sustain enthusiasm and renew energy. Taking a moment to purposefully recognize the commitment it took to succeed and celebrate both the action and the result energizes and motivates. Celebrating success fuels the mind, propels people toward even higher goals and paves the way for the next great accomplishment. It's a vitally important transition step which is missing in far too many workplaces.

Most managers consider celebrating success a frivolous waste of time, and it can be when it is applied poorly or insincerely. Applied properly, celebration is never a waste of time. Celebration is about appreciation, recognition and earned reward. It comes in many forms and it need not take a lot of time or cost any money. For those who have not spent much time celebrating their own successes or the successes of others, taking this step will require some creative thought, but the return is well worth it.

If the goal of business is to get the highest return, keeping the workforce engaged and performing at their highest capacity needs to be a top priority which means understanding what drives the workforce. It means creating an environment that brings out the very best in each member, and rewarding both honest effort and accomplishment in meaningful ways to inspire even greater accomplishments. That is influence in action which is exactly what it will take to ensure that the great power shift, which organizations around the world must face, is beneficial to both the individuals driving the shift and to organizations.

Managing a power shift is rather like a surfer riding a giant wave. Great surfers know to head straight into the wave and just at the point where the wave is about to engulf them, they make an adjustment that allows them to blend and flow with the irresistible force of that wave so the wave picks them up and takes them along with it in a most enjoyable and exhilarating way. They know that trying to resist the force of a great wave would be futile and dangerous, where blending and flowing with it uses the force to advantage.

Awareness is always the first step to effective change. Understanding is the second and clarity the third. Leaders who develop these three assets will be prepared to blend and flow, and take full advantage of changes as they occur.

Awareness of the scope of the power shift we are at the genesis of, and of the fact that it is an inevitable, irresistible force which must be mastered, will give leaders the opportunity to prepare for what lies ahead.

Understanding what is driving the change will help leaders focus their efforts on the right things so they don't waste time and energy, and are able to keep pace with the speed at which this great change is happening.

Clarity around what it will take to be a positive influence through this shift will empower leaders to effectively adjust so they are able to ride that great wave and deftly guide businesses, governments, societies, and the people who populate them, to great new heights.

What happens when an irresistible force meets an influential leader? *Brilliant, world-changing breakthroughs!*

Our dilemma is that we hate change and love it at the same time; what we really want is for things to remain the same, but get better.

Sydney J. Harris

Great leaders keep what has lasting value the same, while making what needs to change better.

Sherry Buffington

ABOUT THE AUTHORS

 **Sherry Buffington, PhD,** is a psychologist, researcher and pioneer in the field of human potential. She has been providing leaders and entrepreneurs with cutting-edge tools and fast, effective methods for getting the best from themselves and their people since 1984.

Through extensive research into intrinsic motivators, generational values, basic drivers of performance and core factors for sustained success, she has developed exceptionally effective tools, methods and programs for eliminating barriers to success and keeping people of every generation engaged and performing to their highest potential.

Sherry is the originator and co-developer of the highly acclaimed *CORE Multidimensional Awareness Profile* (CORE MAP) and the CORE *Personal Effectiveness Profile* (CORE PEP), the developer of the Applied Intrinsic Motivation (AIM) method and creator of many top rated leadership, employee performance and sales success programs. She has authored and co-authored several books on leadership including *Exiting Oz: How the New Generation Workforce is Changing the Face of Business Forever* and *What Cheese? A Leader's Guide to Saying What You Mean to Get What You Want.*

She is the founder of Star Performance Systems, a training, coaching and consulting firm providing cutting-edge tools and game-changing strategies for developing high performance leaders and teams.

The cutting-edge tools and strategies she has developed provide deep, meaningful insights and actionable, measurable results which have contributed to powerful breakthroughs and unprecedented growth for hundreds of organizations, leaders and key employees around the globe. Sherry's focus is on providing leaders and key players with the means to tap into the core factors which drive performance and produce highly motivated, self-driven, star-quality people who consistently outperform their counterparts. Her clients range from small entrepreneurial enterprises to Fortune 100 corporations.

Marc Schwartz has traveled the globe training, coaching and consulting with corporate leaders, managers, and sales professionals for more than thirty years helping them identify and build on the intrinsic motivation that truly drives each person to reach their best both personally and professionally. Additionally, he has trained whole teams and organizations on how to increase results through coaching, leadership and advanced sales skills.

Marc is a highly acclaimed speaker and trainer who actively involves the audience in his presentations through the use of experiential learning techniques and applicable stories. Groups regularly report Marc as high energy and able to have audiences laughing one minute and learning some powerful skills and life lessons the next.

Since 1988, Marc has built a successful consulting practice and several direct sales organizations. He is a founder of SpectraComm and co-founder of Star Performance Systems, training, coaching and consulting firms focused on providing leaders and their teams with cutting-edge tools and programs for getting the best from people.

Marc has presented keynotes, seminars and workshops to over 50,000 people in thirty-eight countries on such topics as Generational Leadership, Coaching, Communication Styles, Sales, Key Account Management, Conflict Resolution and Team Development.

He is the co-author of Power Shift and the author of The Totally Engaged Audience, an eBook on fearless presentations. He has written multiple articles on: training effectiveness, coaching, leadership strategies, emotional intelligence, authentic selling, and how to more fully engage your workforce.

Marc has a BBA in Management and is certified as a Clinical Hypnotherapist, Corporate Coach, NLP Practitioner and Master CORE MAP Facilitator.

Mastering Change

While a rapidly changing world affects all organizations in similar ways, we understand that your challenges and goals are unique to your organization so the solutions we deliver are always *custom-tailored* to you. We never use a one-size-fits-all approach. We get to know you and your company so we fully understand your vision and goals, the challenges you are facing, and the direction you envision so we can provide you with laser-focused solutions.

Through our highly acclaimed *Pulse Point Diagnostic System* we can provide you with an accurate diagnostic of your company's overall health, identify your key players, and provide tools and strategies for creating a culture that will attract and retain highly engaged, self-motivated, high performance people who are dedicated to your success.

We have many years of experience delivering real and measurable outcomes to leaders, key personnel, and teams. We utilize some of the finest developmental tools available anywhere, and we guarantee satisfaction.

Let Us Introduce You To:

- *Pulse Point*™, our highly acclaimed diagnostic system for determining the overall health of your organization and the engagement level of your employees in real time.

- *Applied Intrinsic Motivation*™ (AIM), is an advanced system for developing dedicated, highly motivated, self-driven employees directed toward the achievement of organizational goals.

- *CORE Assessments*™, unmatched for depth, accuracy and highly predictive measures including emotional intelligence. Core assessments are a key tool in tracking and measuring individual development and progress.

Contact Us

Sherry@starperformancesystems.com

Marc@starperformancesystems.com

Website: www.starperformancesystems.com

TESTIMONIALS

"As Director of Employee Training and Organizational Development for my company, I have used Dr. Buffington's services on numerous occasions. The results have always validated why her services are so valuable to the success of our employees, executives and the company in general.

During one of our most memorable and effective engagements, Dr. Buffington and her team were asked to help turn around one of our most important yet least effective, and highly dysfunctional, organizations. In a relatively short period of time the assistance and guidance provided to the organization and my department resulted in a complete and phenomenal turnaround. Customers now routinely comment on the effective way our employees support them. Attrition was reduced to zero, employee morale significantly improved and employee effectiveness went through the roof.

I encourage any decision maker who is not experiencing the maximum performance of her/his organization's employees to contact Dr. Buffington and her Star Performance team for immediate assistance. Your return on investment will be significant."

Wim H. Wetzel PHD/SPHR
NEC America (2011)

"I have worked with countless instruments that provide information about an individual based on their responses to a series of questions. I even completed my doctorate on one. I was skeptical, then, when I first heard of the CORE MAP and I believed it to be a watered down version of other more substantial instruments. Imagine my shock, then, when I found this profile to be amazingly accurate and on-point for me. I heartily recommend it to anyone who wants to know more about themselves or wants to address long-standing issues that may be standing in the way of their personal effectiveness."

Ollie Malone, Jr., Ph.D.
President, Olive Tree Assoc.

"Sherry's program was a huge benefit for NEC. We used CORE MAP regularly to sort through job candidates to find the right fit and behaviors to match a job assignment. We also administered the CORE MAP assessment to existing employees to define and address issues with job performance. It is very valuable as a tool to improve performance and prevent costly hiring mistakes. Sherry's programs are brilliant. Her recommandations have transformed several dapartments in my division and saved NEC thousands of dollars. Both management and the employees have been very pleased with the results. The key here was that with her help, we were able to diagnose problems and provide solutions. Bottom line, we saved many good employees; some by developing them to their highest potential and some by being able to see that they were just in a job that did not fit their style and reassign them to more suitsble jobs. Employees were happy to uncover the source of their anxiety or stress and release it, and NEC was able to fill positions with better-suited candidates."

Scott Espy
Training Director, NEC

The CORE MAP and the follow-up coaching was "just what the Dr. ordered". It was extraordinarily insightful and effective in validating my potential and discovering insights into my passion and motivation. Seeing the depth of this assessment, I realize that other assessments don't go far enough. CORE MAP not only revealed my strengths and abilities, it also raised my awareness of personal and professional liabilities and provided specific feedback that helped me get to the next level in my career. This instrument "hit the nail right on the head."

Dale Perryman
President, Center for Organizational Learning

ROI

Our goal for every client is a significant return on investment. Studies show that the greatest and longest lasting returns occur when the core of an organization, its people, are developed to their highest potential. The value of that approach is repeatedly demonstrated through the returns reported by our client companies and through research which consistently returns results such as:

- Stock portfolios comprised of companies that spend aggressively on employee development outperformed the S&P 500 by 17-35% during 2003. (Bassi and McMurrer 2004)

- In 2014 revenues increased by an average of 22.2 percent for the Fortune 100 Best Companies to Work For and, according to the Bureau of Labor Statistics, these same companies added new employees at rate that was five times higher than the national average indicating substantial growth. (Fortune Magazine, May 2015)

- Companies that use professional coaching for business reasons have seen a median return on their investment of **7 times** their initial investment, according to a study commissioned by ICF, and conducted by Pricewaterhousecoopers and Association Resource Centre, Inc. (International Coach Federation, April 2009)

- According to calculations prepared by Merrill C. Anderson, a professor of clinical education at Drake University, effective external training and coaching programs earn an average of **5.2x return on investment** and significant intangible benefits. When the financial benefits from employee retention was factored, in the ROI increased to **7.8x the initial investment.** (Anderson, July 2005)

Bibliography

Akerson, Daniel F. Leaders Online Magazine interview, July 2013. http://www.leadersmag.com/issues/2013.3_Jul/toc20133.html

Amabile, Fisher and Pillemer. IDEO's Culture of Helping, Harvard Business Review, Jan 2014

Anderson, Merrill C. PhD. Case Study on the Return on Investment of Executive Development; MetrixGlobal, LLC, July 22, 2005)

Aratti, Sampatkumar B. HR Dept, People Matter, September 19, 2013

Bart, Mary. College Students Unplugged: 24 Hours without Media Brings Feelings of Boredom, Isolation, Anxiety; Faculty Focus, Faculty Focus, May 27, 2010.

Bassi, Laurie and McMurrer, Daniel. How's Your Return on People? Harvard Business Review, March 2004

Beck, Don and Cowan, Christopher. Spiral Dynamics: Mastering Values, Leadership, and Change; Wiley/Blackwell 1996

Bell, Judy W. PHR. High Emotional Intelligence: What EQ Brings to the Workplace, HR Magazine Online, 2014

Carnegie, Dale. How to Win Friends and Influence People; Simon and Schuster, 1936, Page 23

Capodagli, Bill/Jackson. The Disney Way: Harnessing the Management Secrets of Disney in Your Company; McGraw-Hill 2003

Collins, Jim. Good to Great;

Cross, Jay. Low Hanging Fruit is Tasty; Chief Learning Officer Magazine, 2006

Csikszentmihalyi, Mihaly. Flow: The Psychology of Optimal Experience; 2008, HarperCollins

Dychtwald, Ken, Erickson, Tamara and Morrison, Robert. Workforce Crisis; Harvard Business School Press 2006

Ericsson, Anders K., Prietula, Michael, and Cokely, Edward. The Making of an Expert, Harvard Business Review, Managing for the Long Term, July-August 2007.

Ericsson, Anders K., Krampe, Ralf and Tesch-Romer, Clemens. The Role of Deliberate Practice in the Acquisition of Expert Performance; Psychological Review, 1993, Vol. 100. No. 3, pages 363-406)

Gallup, Inc. State of the American Workplace, 2013

Gladwell, Malcolm. Outliers, Little, Brown & Co. 2008, Pg 38

Goldstone, Jack A. Youth Bulges and the Social Conditions of Rebellion, World Politics Review, Tuesday, Nov. 20, 2012

Goleman, Daniel. Primal Leadership: Realizing the Power of Emotion; Harvard Business School Press 2002

Gregersen, Hal. Behind the Scenes of a Great Turnaround, MIT Sloan School of Management Newsroom, 2014

Hannan, Caleb. Dish Network, the Meanest Company in America, Bloomberg Business; January 2013

Hathaway, Bill. Even in the Healthy, Stress Causes the Brain to Shrink; Yale News, January 2012

Hoffman, Michael and Jamal, Amaney. The Youth and the Arab Spring Cohort Differences and Similarities, Middle East Law and Governance 4 (2012) 168–188, Princeton University

Howe, Neil and Strauss, William. Millennials Rising: The Next Great Generation; Random House, 2000

Huffington Post. Charitable Giving: 75% Of Millennials Donated Money to Causes In 2011 (STUDY); 05/02/2013 (Author not provided)

Huffington Post. JC Penney Exec Admits Its Employees Harbored Enormous YouTube Addiction; February 25, 2012

International Coach Federation. ICF Global Coaching Client Study, PricewaterhouseCoopers, April 2009

Jackson, Eric. Top Ten Reasons Why Large Companies Fail to Keep Their Best Talent; Forbes.Com Magazine, December 2011

Jacobus, Casey. It's Not Racin'; It's Performance, Greater Charlotte Biz Online; May 2009

Keller, Scott and Aiken, Carolyn. The Inconvenient Truth About Change Management, [Academia.edu, August, 2000)

Kingkade, Tyler. 5 Reasons Millennials Are Going To Save the World (We Hope), The Huffington Post, November 05, 2013

Knab, Christopher. Changes in the Way Music is Sold Over the Last 30 Years; Fourfront Media & Music, January 2008.)

Kot, Greg. Today's music industry: Not the same old song and dance; LA Times, September 06, 2009

Miller, Laurie. 2014 State of the Industry Report: Spending on Employee Training Remains a Priority; Association for Talent Development Magazine, November, 2014

Farfan, Barbara. JCPenney Founder, James Cash Penney: Quotations About Principles in Business, Retail Industry News, 2015

Schwartz, Tony. Why You Hate Work; New York Times, May 2014

Schawbel, Dan. 74 of the Most Interesting Facts About the Millennial Generation, June 25, 2013, Dan Schwabel Workplace Trends

Semler, Ricardo. Maverick: The Success Story Behind the World's Most Unusual Workplace, Warner Books, 1995

Sinek, Simon. 2009-09-23. Start with Why: How Great Leaders Inspire Everyone to Take Action, (Kindle Locations 1596-1606). Penguin Group US. Kindle Edition.

Spiegel, Alix. Struggle for Smarts? How Eastern and Western Cultures Tackle Learning, NPR.org, November 2012.

Urban, Tim. Wait, but Why, September 15, 2013, Huffington Post http://www.huffingtonpost.com/wait-but-why/generation-y-unhappy_b_3930620.html

Winograd and Hais. Millennials Lead the Nation in Service to Our Country, August 2009, NDN.org

Zenoff, David B. The Soul of the Organization: How to Ignite Employee Engagement and Productivity at Every Level, December 2012, Apress

Index

A

Abdicators **79**, **80**, **129**, **130**

Acres of Diamonds **55**

AIM **50**, **141**, **159**, **167**, **168**, **169**

Akerson, Daniel **140**, **173**

American Society for Training and Development **73**

Anderson, Dr. William H. **31**

Anderson, Merrill C. **172**

Applied Intrinsic Motivation **50**, **141**, **159**, **164**, **167**

Appreciative Inquiry **156**, **157**

Aratti, Sampatkumar B. **146**

B

Baby Boomers **2**, **11**, **15**, **23**, **33**, **34**, **38**, **41**, **46**, **53**, **54**, **57**, **113**, **115**, **116**

BASE **45**, **51**

Burnout **62**, **64**, **120**

C

Capacity **6**, **59**, **72**, **74**, **163**, **164**

Carnegie, Dale **157**

Change management **11**

Collins, Jim **5**, **135**, **136**, **137**, **173**

Competence **67**, **74**, **75**, **76**

Conscious Intent **69**

CORE **9**, **10**, **48**, **49**, **50**, **75**, **76**, **136**, **137**, **164**, **167**, **168**, **170**, **171**

Costco **4, 42, 53, 101, 102**

Cromwell, Russell **55**

Csikszentmihalyi, Mihaly **13, 138**

D

Dallas Cowboys **127, 128**

Dent, Harry S. **118**

Disney, Walt **93, 94, 127, 157**

Douglas McGregor **27**

E

Emotion **174**

Emotional Intelligence **75, 173**

Employee Engagement **30, 175**

Enforcers **79, 80, 129, 130**

Ericsson **146, 147, 155, 174**

Ericsson, K. Anders **146**

Exiting OZ **89**

F

Flow **13, 138, 173**

Free the Children **153**

G

Gallup **9, 35, 53, 80, 96, 139, 174**

Generation X **11, 22, 23, 34, 41, 46, 53, 54, 57, 81, 96, 104, 153**

Genghis Khan **19, 20, 87, 110**

Gen X **3, 15, 42, 54, 153**

Glassdoor **56, 95, 159**

Goleman, Daniel **135**

H

Herman Trend Alert **139**

High Potential **65**

I

ICMPA study **97**

IDEO **112, 124, 173**

Influencers **79, 80, 81, 130**

Intention **7**

J

Jellison, Jerald **160**

Johnson, Ron **88**

Jones, Jerry **127, 128**

K

Kaizen **145**

Kelleher, Herb **4, 5, 127**

Kielburger, Craig **153**

Klopp, Breon **162**

Knab, Christopher **100**

Kot, Greg **99**

L

Lowe, Jack **57**

M

McGregor, Douglas **27**

Meme **113**

Millennial Index **108**

Millennials **vi, 1, 2, 3, 4, 15, 17, 22, 23, 24, 26, 30, 31, 37, 38, 39, 40, 41, 42, 46, 53, 54, 57, 73, 81, 85, 95, 96, 97, 98, 99, 104, 105, 106, 107, 108, 109, 110, 114,**

115, 116, 117, 118, 131, 132, 145, 149, 151, 152, 153, 154, 158, 159, 174, 175

N

NASCAR **162**

Nayar, Vineet **84**

Nierenberg, Roger **154**

O

Organizational pH Litmus Test **91**

P

Pearson **142**

Penney, James Cash **88, 175**

Performance Matrix **61, 73**

Porath **142**

Primal Leadership **135, 174**

Proficiency Trap **62**

R

Rogers Innovation Adoption Curve **101**

S

Sarillo, Nick **132**

Schwab, Charles **157**

Self-awareness **75, 141**

Self-management **140, 141**

Semco **26, 27, 117, 127, 151**

Semler, Ricardo **26, 117, 127, 151**

Southwest Airlines **4, 5, 127**

Spiral Dynamics **22, 113, 114, 173**

Star Performers **62, 64**

Stigler, Jim **110**

Strauss, William **116**

Structured Freedom **81, 120**

Struggler **65**

Subconscious Function **69**

T

Traditionalists **23, 38, 46, 53, 54, 97, 110, 113**

Traditionals **11, 38, 41**

V

VIP Leader **83, 138, 154**

W

Walmart **56, 102, 103**

Weiner, Jeff **158**

Welch, Jack **16**

X

Xerox **144**

Z

Zenoff, David B. **30**